Praise f[illegible]

As parts coordinator for Holiday World of Houston, I hear almost daily from full-timers and part-timers of their RV adventures—and their misadventures. The tales told by Anita and her friends represent well all the extraordinary stories I've heard of RV life. For many of us creeping up on retirement, Tales from the Road will turn up the excitement to discover North America.

Anita's listings of great parks and the contact information she provides take the guesswork out of finding the right campgrounds. Thanks, Anita, for writing another must-have book for RVers. I will be sure to tell our customers about it.

— Chuck Willimann, Parts Coordinator, Holiday World of Houston, Katy, TX

As someone who always thought going RVing sounded like vacation freedom, Tales from the Road is truly appealing. Funny, eye-opening, and packed with great tips and insights, this book will take you from the bookshelf and easy chair to the open road.

— Susan Allen, General Manager, Borders Books & Music, St. Louis, MO

Anita and her husband, Paul, and their many road friends share with us the humor and adventures of life on the road. Laugh along with them at the mishaps, experience the wonderful people they meet along the way, and learn valuable technical tips and interesting places to visit. Long-time RVers will enjoy this book, and it can serve as a light, amusing, helpful introduction to the RV life.

— Marcella Gauthier, Book Editor, Escapees Magazine, Livingston, TX

As new trailer owners (inspired by Anita's first book), my husband and I could relate to the first-timer stories. We've experienced similar incidents, and we feel better knowing we're in good company. Both of Anita's books provide lots of helpful information for novice as well as experienced RVers and trailer enthusiasts. We look forward to the adventures that lie ahead.

— Karen and Don Conley, newbie RV adventurers

I first encountered Anita Henehan at a Camping World in the form of her first book, How to Run Away from Home After 50. I was one of the thousands who wanted out of the rat race—to be able to do what I wanted to do before I couldn't do it anymore. In her book I found a road map of sorts, direction in the form of stories and experiences. The second time I met Anita, I'd been living the dream, traveling the U.S. in a motor home, and I was a work camper at Sun-N-Fun RV Resort. Imagine my surprise to meet the author who'd set me on my course. She was collecting stories for this book. I recommend Tales from the Road to anyone looking for a road map—or just a good read.

— Gary Riedel, Sun-N-Fun RV Resort, Sarasota, Florida
Travel Far...Dream Big...Live Well

Author (and RVer) Anita Henehan has done it again. Her second book, Tales from the Road: Adventures of Mid-Life Runaways, is a delightfully engaging collection of first-hand stories and anecdotes, as diverse as the couples who share them. Whether you're a full-timer, part-timer, or still considering, you're sure to be inspired and entertained by these remarkably honest—and often very funny—"tales from the road."

— Randy Puckett, Marketing/Communications Editor, Monaco RV

Tales from the Road

Adventures of Mid-Life Runaways

Anita S. Henehan

Table of Contents

Dedication

I want to dedicate this book to my husband, Paul. I've had experiences and seen places I never could or would have without him. I'm so grateful for having him in my life and for all the help he's given me in writing this, my second book, as well as my first book, *How to Run Away from Home After 50,* about the RV life.

I feel like I'm the luckiest person in the world to have married my best friend. Thanks a million, honey.

Acknowledgments

I would like to thank the many people who have helped bring *Tales from the Road* to fruition. My wonderful RV friends and generous contributors have enriched this book with their stories and expanded its scope. My insightful book coach and good friend, Linda Nash, once again believed in me and helped me bring my ideas together in an orderly fashion. My editor, Barbara McNichol, and her associate, Peggy Henrikson, brought further clarity and polish to the finished product. As with my first book, *How to Run Away from Home After 50*, the cover concept was developed by my friend Jim Schomaker, designed by Karen Saunders, and illustrated by Fred Eyer. I'm grateful to you all for your time, talent, and caring.

Introduction

When I wrote *How to Run Away from Home After 50*, it was just the beginning as it turns out. My readers encouraged me to keep writing, and in this second book, *Tales from the Road*, several of them share their own stories. I hope this book will keep you from missing the unique, out-of-the-way places we've found and prevent you from making the mistakes we've made. Of course, I also hope you love the fun, funny, and poignant stories we have to tell.

A dear friend gave my husband and me an inspiring perspective on our adventures when we stopped to see him on our way home from a trip. Father Tom Meyer is the pastor of St. Anthony's Catholic Church in Effingham, Illinois. For years, we were his surrogate parents while he was a student at Kenrick Seminary in St. Louis.

Father Tom offered profound words of wisdom when I told him about our travels and writing this book. Coming from a man of God, I was not surprised. He said, "What you're doing takes the faith of God because you're doing something different from what you're accustomed to. Be flexible, with faith and a heart of adventure." He also told us we're "finding our Jerusalem" in every place and in every day of our lives.

Father Tom's theme winds its way throughout *Tales from the Road*. When you "find your Jerusalem" wherever you are, you've found pure happiness, peace, excitement, and enthusiasm. I wish such happiness for everyone who reads this book. You can have your Jerusalem, too. We're living proof—and we're so grateful!

Anita S. Henehan
February 2010

Chapter 1

First-Timers: Having Fun—or Not

Getting started in the RV world is always exciting—a new adventure! Most veteran RVers remember that feeling—the eagerness to load up and get on the road for the first time. The RV life is certainly a learning experience finding out what to do—and what not to do. We make mistakes, we find help, and we meet the most wonderful people as we travel down the highways. Fellow adventurers who've contributed to this book come from many places—Florida, Pennsylvania, New Jersey, Indiana, North Carolina, Missouri, and Michigan to name a few. We're all looking for the same thing—whether we have small trailers or large motor coaches—and we all love to come together to share our fun, stories, and adventures. I've included my stories and theirs to get your motor running!

The Day We Picked Up Our First Coach

Anita Henehan

My husband Paul and I picked her up on Friday in Rockford, Illinois, around 3:30 in the afternoon. But it wasn't until 6:30 that we got through with orientation on how to operate our new home on wheels. Finally, we rolled out of the showroom. We just had the hitch installed on our Chevy Tahoe and had a lot to learn about that, too. We also learned how to "dump" the black water, fill the fresh water tank, and many other new things. My mind was in a whirl.

After our first long day on the road, we were hungry, tired, and still a bit confused about our new RV. I opted for staying at the Holiday Inn, but Paul was adamant about staying in our new coach. He declared that after spending all that money, we were going to camp no matter what. We decided to "try" to camp at a park close by. It was raining, freezing cold, and very dark. Did I mention I was hungry?

Somehow we found the park and, after some confusion and fumbling, we got set up. Finally, we ate dinner in our new camper at about ten-thirty. We crashed happily into bed somewhere around midnight.

It has got to get better than this, I thought. Little did I know that this was the first night of many more exciting and wonderful adventures to come.

Our First Big RV Adventure

Sue Goulet

Day 1. Our first RV trip started out well. We were on our way to Urbanna, Virginia, for an RV rally, and had no problems until we came to a toll booth. The cars wouldn't let us into the truck lane, so we had no choice but to try to squeeze through the toll lane for regular cars. Now that was scary!! Without an inch to spare, my husband, Norm, began yelling because he couldn't reach down to get the ticket. Like I could help? At this point, the people behind us were piling up and horns were blaring. I finally said to Norm, "Just drive through and we'll pay at the other end."

Then the girl from the other booth walked over and told us to open the door. Norm asked her to slip the ticket through the window. At that point, she replied rather angrily,

"Do you know you're in the wrong lane?" I thought Norm was going to somehow manage to get out and kill her! Finally, we were able to squeeze through and go on.

Let me tell you, car drivers simply do not care about RV drivers. Here we were, driving a 38-foot RV and pulling an Explorer truck. So we were looonnnggg. But sorry, cars come first.

Well, we made it through the first day of nine and a half hours of driving—and gee, no bruises on either one of us. We decided to stay at a Flying J travel station, where they let people sleep overnight in their RVs. We drove into the lot, but it was full. We decided to go around the building to leave so we wouldn't have to back out. (In case you didn't know, you can't back up an RV when you're towing a car or the front wheels of the car will jackknife.) No dice. The dumpster was in the way. Norm had to get out and unhitch the Explorer so we could back it up and back up the RV. Then he had to re-hitch. Oh happy day!

Then I noticed a Cracker Barrel restaurant across the street. I checked the *Next EXIT* book, which says what's off every exit in the U.S. It did indicate a Cracker Barrel at that exit, and the letters were in red, which means RVs can spend the night. So I said to Norm, "Hey, let's go there." After we'd crossed to the Cracker Barrel lot, Norm told me to get out and ask the manager if we could stay in the parking lot. The manager had never heard of this, but he agreed because it said so in the book. "Are you eating here?" he asked. "But of course," I replied. After nine and a half hours, I would have eaten anything anywhere. The manager told us to drive around back where the buses park. Of course we had to unhitch the truck again. But, hey, GREAT!!! At least we had a place to sleep.

Day 2. The second day went pretty well, except we had to stop at a rest area because I was a little nauseous from the day before from driving on those cement highways that have bumps in them. We got some Dramamine at the rest area, non-drowsy, of course. WRONG!!! As we were driving, I kept falling asleep, and I was the copilot and direction girl. Norm had to keep waking me up to ask where we were. Heck, I didn't care; I was in Lala Land. I read the ingredients on the Dramamine box. Oops. I had obviously bought the wrong pills.

I decided to get up and make us a snack while Norm was driving to wake myself up. As I was standing there trying to balance, Norm hit the brakes. Out came the slide-out table we'd forgotten to lock. OUCH!! Now that woke me up.

I hobbled back to my seat and made it the rest of the way to Urbanna. Ahhh! Finally here. This is a nice place.

I figured that while Norm was doing all the outside stuff, I would set up inside for cocktail hour. At that point, nine in the morning would have been a good cocktail time for me. But at four o'clock, I was ready. I opened the liquor cabinet and a big wine bottle crashed to the floor smashing into a million pieces. Red wine flowed everywhere. I stood barefoot in the middle of it yelling HELP! Norm walked in and said, "What did you do now?"

We finally got the ceramic floor cleaned up, but I did notice the wine slowly snaking its way under the cabinets. Well, that was better than staining the carpet.

Okay forget the wine. Now we're bringing out the Southern Comfort Manhattans, three cherries and all. It's 86 degrees and very humid. Oh this is so much fun. We finally finished off the day and settled in with the group of all Holiday

Rambler RVs headed for the rally in Virginia. Campers are so friendly. We made it through the night. The next day we were off to Williamsburg.

Norm decided while I was getting ready for happy hour again, he would connect the water filter under the sink. All of a sudden, it was like Hampton Beach filling our rig. Norm was yelling to me to shut off the water but I had no idea what he was talking about. After he figured it out, we finally got it all cleaned up, soggy carpet and all. No new filter.

I walked around that night and was talking to some of the other campers who had rigs like ours. I told them about our experience and they said they knew what had happened. They'd be right over to help. It turned out the filter was defective. Oh well, another floor washing. That ceramic tile was shining. Fortunately, we were still able to laugh. We were the only people from New Hampshire, and because it was a Virginia rally, everyone knew who we were.

We did have a great time. It was our first experience and, yes, one we will remember. One trip down and lots more to go.

Leaping Lizard!

John Carlson

Four years ago I took a new bride. We had known each another 40 years before that, but had just gotten back together after a year of emailing. As a motor home person, I was concerned about how my wife, Marcia, would take to the camping life. After a honeymoon cruise to the eastern Caribbean, Marcia and I took our first RV trip to Kissimmee, Florida. It started out well.

Then one night during the second week while we were in bed, something plopped on my wife's chest. She screamed and ran into the living room. After 40 minutes of spraying for "bugs," I convinced her to come back to bed.

The next morning, she asked me what the seam in the floor under the bed was for. I said, "Oh, that's for storage." I lifted the bed. Wouldn't you know, a Florida lizard was sitting on top of the spare pillow. Hysterics ensued.

I took Marcia outside to show her the entrance to the storage area under the bed and asked her to wait while I went inside to jiggle things around and see if the gingko (lizard) would come out. More hysterics! She said the lizard came flying out like his life depended on it.

While Marcia was carrying on, a neighbor came over and asked what was happening. "Did you find my pet?" he wanted to know.

"What pet?" replied Marcia. "Oh," said the neighbor, "I have a black snake living under my motor home." Even more hysterics!! "Don't worry," the neighbor assured her. "Black snakes are harmless and helpful. They keep the rattlesnakes away."

It took the strongest sales pitch of my life to keep my new partner as a camping buddy.

Watch Out for Toll Booths!

Ernie Menold

We were traveling in our first motor home on our way to Florida. My wife, Helen, was driving and I sat in the passenger seat. As we approached a toll booth, Helen didn't realize it but she was half in her lane and half in the next lane. The eyes of the woman in the booth suddenly got wider and wider. As panic flashed crossed her face, she shouted and waved, "Get over! Get over!" Helen didn't realize that motor homes are wider than you think. After that, I took over the driving. It probably saved both of us—and saved a few toll booth attendants from panic attacks.

A Family Adventure

Tanny Latuska

Al and I paid for our new 29-foot motor home one Saturday, packed up on Sunday, and took off on Monday with our two preteen children. We picked up both my parents and my husband's parents to join us on a three-week trip to California, Oregon, Washington, and Canada.

Fortunately, a friend lent us his pop-up camper so we could all sleep comfortably. You see, my father could "rattle the timbers" with his snoring. We decided my parents and the children would sleep in the motor home while my husband's parents and he and I would sleep in the pop-up to get some real zzzs. My husband was designated to be the only driver.

On this trip, Al and I wanted to attend the graduation of one of our eight godchildren, see some sights, and provide pleasure to our parents. They'd worked hard all their lives but could never afford to travel much. When we reached Rapid City, South Dakota, Al decided to check in with his secretary at the supermarket he managed back home. You know, just in case. Thank goodness he did. The store was fine, but the motor home dealer was concerned because our check had bounced! We had just changed banks, but I hadn't yet changed checkbooks and, without thinking, I had written the check on the old account. Fortunately, we had lived in that city a long time and people knew us. Al's secretary made some calls of explanation. Money got transferred, our check cleared, and a crisis was averted.

After visiting friends and attending the graduation ceremonies, we left for Portland, Oregon, where we took in the Rose Festival. What an experience seeing thousands of roses. They were all so beautiful, I don't know how judges could pick the winners. Then we journeyed on to Seattle where the children were impressed with the famous landmark, the Space Needle, with its revolving restaurant high up. Children seem to like anything that moves.

From Washington, we headed east to Glacier National Park. Upon arrival at the Park entrance, we registered at the booth. My husband thought our rig might be too long with the pop-up behind, but the attendant cleared us to go. However, after we'd driven a third of the way through and encountered a few "hairy" turns, a patrol officer stopped us. He wanted to ticket us for having a setup that was too long. But after calling back to the entrance and being told the woman at the entrance had cleared us, the officer relented on the ticket but insisted we turn around and go back. Now, if you've ever been in this park, you know about the hairpin curves and the extremely narrow main road. It's a task maneuvering the straightaway, let alone turning around a big motor home towing a pop-up camper. Shocked, my husband asked how we could ever accomplish this feat. The officer replied he would lead us to an area where we could turn around. After some serious maneuvering, Al succeeded. The dead-silent passengers were then able to relax their white knuckles and breathe again.

All in all, we greatly enjoyed the trip. We didn't get to see all of Glacier National Park, but what we did see was special and highly recommended.

Fried to Frozen

Sandy and John Fanello

After years of talking about going on the road full time, we finally sold our house and had to move out in two short weeks. Whew! Over 50 years of collecting "stuff." What to do? We rented a six-by-eight storage unit to store the can't-live-without stuff, held a major garage sale, and sold all our furniture.

We were so excited! It was our first day as full-time RVers. Feeling upbeat and happy with the sale price of our home, we looked forward to seeing the USA from our Class A 38-foot RV. However, before beginning our great adventure, we stayed at a nearby lake campground to tie up loose ends. Upon our arrival, we soon discovered we had a problem with our satellite receiver.

Being positive people, we decided that "things" just happen and took the RV to a local dealer. Because the dealer had to order several items, we returned to the same campground to wait for the parts to arrive.

But this is not the end of the story. The very next night, the temperature dropped to 28 degrees. Unfortunately, we hadn't unhooked from the main water source. It totally froze and left our hose one solid line of ice. No water the next morning. Okay, maybe we have a lot to learn being "newbies." We're still looking forward to heading down the road. Stay tuned! We're excited.

Chapter 2

Full-Timers

After a year or two or ten of being on the road, you learn the ropes and pitfalls in RV traveling. You also find rare opportunities and unique places that most people don't even know exist. It may be working in a national park, going to RV rallies, or a myriad of other things and places you can share with the newbies you meet along the way.

If you're new to RV travel, listen to these seasoned travelers. They will help make your next adventure even greater.

Full-Timers Delight

Dan Miller

Technically, we "live" somewhere we've never been. I'll explain this riddle later.

My wife, Laraine, our golden retriever, and I live full time in a 32-foot fifth-wheel trailer with two slides. Everything we own is inside (or underneath in storage). This "upgrade" has been home for the past 12 months. I say upgrade because before we moved up to a fifth wheel, we were in a 26-foot motor home with no slides.

People who know me call me a minimalist, but I prefer to think in terms of unencumbered and unstressed. This lifestyle has allowed us to "semi-retire" over the years while being relatively young. We still have to work, but we now have the luxury to pick and choose where, when, how long, and how hard we work.

After a long, successful career in Indiana, we decided to start over in Florida. Because both of us love warm weather, this seemed to be a good idea. Only our dog wasn't happy about leaving cold weather behind. We had carefully picked out a spot during one of our many vacation trips, so we weren't settling down blind. This worked out well. Florida is a great place to live (especially if you like fresh fruits and vegetables year-round), but our wanderlust eventually caught up with us. It was time to travel, and everyone we knew advised us to "do it while you're young."

We had heard about working while RVing, and we got prepared to try it out for ourselves. We sold our house and bought the aforementioned 26-foot motor home. Our first experience turned out better than expected (beginners luck!), and we found ourselves working in the midst of Grand Teton and Yellowstone National Parks. The RV sites were first rate and we could look out our back window into a forest of lodge pole pines. Wildlife showed up everywhere. Once, we almost backed into a buffalo leaving the employee laundry after doing our first loads. Moose, elk, mule deer, buffalo, and even an occasional bear were all seen within walking distance, further reinforcing the decision we had made.

After two summers in "paradise" and a nice winter in Phoenix, it was time to look for another winter destination, so we sent a résumé to Forever Resorts, operating in Big Bend National Park in Texas. A month later, we were negotiating our arrival date. Although we originally committed to working the winter season, we spent a full year and a half there, officially trading javelina for moose. (Javelina are animals that look like wild pigs and live in Arizona.)

Eventually Big Bend lost its hold on us, so we decided to go back to the Yellowstone area. After traveling the southeast (where spring lasted three months), we finished our family visits and ended up in Cody, Wyoming. More scenery, more wildlife, another experience, another wonderful location. What a lifestyle.

Alas, winters in Wyoming are not meant for RVs, and an opportunity to live and work in Sarasota, Florida, became available. Again, we lucked out and ended up in a great area full of wildlife, beautiful tropical scenery, and fantastic winter weather. As of this writing, we are nearing the completion of our "southern assignment" and are planning our trip to Alaska. Yes, Alaska is the next destination.

In case you can't tell from this brief story, we're really enjoying this lifestyle and haven't yet tired of life on the road. Oh yeah. I told you I would answer the "riddle" mentioned earlier. Our "permanent" address is Pensacola, Florida, and we've never ever been there.

Wilma and Coy's

Anita Henehan

We had just left St. Louis in our 25-foot trailer with Rend Lake, Illinois, as our first stop as full timers. It was time to do new things. We had heard that fishing was relaxing and fun so Paul and I brought fishing rods with us, although neither of us had ever fished.

After we parked at the campsite in Rend Lake and then relaxed, played golf, and hiked for a few days, we wanted to try our hand at fishing. When we drove around Rend Lake, we saw a sign that said "Wilma and Coy's fishing bait for sale." Yes, that's what we need. We parked and walked into the store, then went up to the young man behind the counter. I told him we were new in the area and didn't know how to fish—could he teach us how to fish?

"First," he said, "you need bait." "What kind do you suggest?" I asked. He pointed to a tank full of crickets. As Paul bent down to look at them, dozens of crickets jumped up and down in the tank. Their smell was horrendous.

"How many crickets do you want?" he asked. "I don't know," I answered. "How many do we need?" He suggested a "cricket hotel," which is a plain box that holds a good many crickets. As we paid for the "cricket hotel," Paul asked, "Where's a good place to fish nearby?" "Under the bridge where fish bite just before dusk." So we drove there, parked by the bridge, and climbed over the rocks loaded down with fishing gear: rods, bobbers, hooks, and, of course, the "cricket hotel."

After we positioned ourselves on the rocks with all our "equipment," Paul opened the box. Low and behold, the "cricket hotel" exploded like a Roman candle. All the crickets jumped out! Picture us chasing these jumping crickets all over the place. We did finally rescue a few to put on our fishing hooks. With great effort, I attempted to cast the rods with the bobbers, the hooks, and the crickets. Every time I tried to cast the rod, I hit the rocks instead of the water, smashing several bobbers. At first we found this rather comical, but after several smashed bobbers, it ceased to be funny!

That day, we did manage to catch two little (and I mean little) fish. Paul filleted them immediately and we fried them back at the coach—our first and last dinner of fish that we'd caught ourselves.

Mercy Ships

Delores Mason

It was the summer of 2004 and our long-time dream of RV-ing to Alaska was finally coming true. We left our home in Florida and camped all along the Mississippi River, even walking across it at the headwaters in northern Minnesota. We traveled across Canada and throughout Alaska, all the while marveling at the beauty of this wonderful country.

As we traveled back toward home, we made our way down through the western state of Washington where we gazed at the Pacific Ocean just as Lewis and Clark had done. We stood in awe of Mount St. Helens, watched the sunset across the Pacific along the Oregon coast, and gazed with amazement at the giant California redwoods and huge trees in Yosemite National Park.

Then we realized that this trip was everything we had hoped for and more. But on our way home to Florida, I happened to read an article in our *Escapees* magazine about an organization in East Texas called Mercy Ships that needed volunteers. My husband, Leslie, and I found the idea of volunteering intriguing. I checked into Mercy Ships and discovered it was a global charity that owns and operates large hospital ships. They transport free medical help to the poor in developing nations. The ships remain in one port for as long as seven months, which allows for long-term projects such as supporting community health, drilling wells, and building schools and clinics. All this accomplished entirely with volunteers!

After speaking with the volunteer coordinator at Mercy Ships, we were accepted as volunteers and parked our RV in the small RV park on the grounds. Even as we drove onto the Mercy Ships' 430-acre campus in the Piney Woods region of East Texas, I sensed an atmosphere of peace. This feeling continued for the weeks we were there. It seemed to us—and to them—that this was God's special timing. Mercy Ships was sponsoring a musical concert, and they had been looking for someone to phone churches and help promote the concert, so that became (literally and figuratively) our calling. Still, we sensed all were appreciated, no matter what job or position we held.

While we were at Mercy Ships, Hurricane Ivan hit Florida and the East Coast with a vengeance. One of the Mercy Ships was docked in Alabama for supplies and had to be evacuated for safety while a skeleton technical crew sailed it out of danger. Most of those who had been living on board came to the International Operations Center (IOC) in East Texas for refuge.

Meanwhile, we got word that our property in Pensacola, Florida, had suffered heavy damage. Our common concern drew us together for support. Relieved to learn that none of our family members were injured, we decided to stay in Texas until the completion of our project.

These weeks at Mercy Ships were some of the most memorable and heartwarming we'd ever experienced—truly a special time and place in our lives. What a perfect ending for an unforgettable trip.

Workamping Fun at YMCA Trout Lodge

Nancy Adkins

My husband, Farrell, and I have been camp hosts in Florida and for six state parks in Missouri. We've also been hosts for the Elderhostel at YMCA Trout Lodge and Camp Lakewood at Potosi, Missouri (collectively known as YMCA of the Ozarks) since 2000. That's where we tried out a new program called Workamping, which allows campers to take on various work projects at the Camp. We chose the minimum timeframe of six weeks with 15 hours a week to make sure we could handle whatever the volunteering might require, being 71 years old and all.

Let me start from when we arrived at Trout Lodge. We warn you that the entrance to the campground isn't marked, and you may drive right by it the first time you go there. The camp doesn't mark it for fear they'll have unwanted visitors. It is well hidden among the trees next to the trout ponds, a natural spring, and the home of a muskrat near the first pond. We saw that muskrat raise its head several times and look around, then go back into its hole. One time, Farrell saw it dive under the water and swim out into the pond.

As part of the Workamping program, I asked to volunteer for arts and crafts and was scheduled for 12 hours a week. I enjoyed my work with the arts and crafts teachers. I helped them fill glue bottles, cut up cardboard, and set up the tables for painting, ceramics, making Super Caps and masks, and other crafts. I cleaned up afterwards, too, which freed those who had been trained to teach. It was so fun to see families create things together.

For the other three hours a week, I was to help Farrell on his hayrides and, later, with the Musical Canoes. You see, Farrell loves to perform. He sings, plays the guitar and harmonica, and imitates his favorite person, Willie Nelson. He always performed on the hayrides and for a time at the Triangle Y Ranch. Farrell also worked at the boat dock, where he helped people who needed life jackets and canoes, paddle boats, sailboats, and so on. He loved this because he got to meet and interact with students from all over the world.

The Musical Canoes program proved to be almost more than we could handle. We were told to take a pontoon over to the other side of the lake with fire wood, a cooler with goodies for s'mores, Farrell's guitar, and a fire starter. The first time we forgot the wood, but Farrell found some leftover wood and lots of dead limbs. The lifeguard brought people in canoes. The first time, we had one family of four people; the second time, we had a group of families—a total of 28 people. Among them, the husbands had attended kindergarten together, and they typically gather once a year. Our sing-along featured requested show tunes, such as "The Sound of Music," which Farrell sang for the group.

One time, weather became a big problem for the Musical Canoes event. We weren't supposed to leave for the other side of the lake if it was thundering, but if it was just cloudy and threatening, we could go on over and wait, so we did. After being there about 10 minutes, we were usually told to come back because the event had been cancelled. We lucked out, though—no real storms.

We found the hayrides to be the most fun. Families from all over the United States met at the beautiful lodge. We had

12 Italians from New York, Florida, Kansas, and St. Louis, and did they love to sing! Farrell needed no preparation for that singalong; he just played. Participating were very young children who didn't know the songs, but they always knew "Twinkle, Twinkle Little Star." We had many lovely sweet solos of that special song.

As a workamper, you're a volunteer, but you get to camp free and meals are furnished at the impressive lodge on the lake. Rather than drive our large truck about three miles by road to the lodge, we decided to ride our bikes. On the bike path, it was only one mile to the lodge and one mile back. That amounted to six miles a day if we ate there three times a day—and we missed very few lodge meals. We stayed in our camper only for a few breakfasts, which indicates how much we enjoyed the meals at the lodge. The biking was great exercise, too. We encountered only one hill, which meant I had to push harder. In cool weather, that would have been fine, but in July, it was hot.

Four sites were reserved for workampers, and we had one on each side of us. They were both long-term workers, but one had to leave early because of family problems. Our Chihuahua, Ci Ci, took well to our site and the camp. She loved the trout ponds and running up and down the trails with me. She also relished chasing the two rabbits that waited in the mornings and again in the evenings for her to chase them back into the woods.

People could volunteer as program workers as well as workampers and teach classes such as riflery, archery, shotgun, crafts, and so on. Other programs were made available for workampers, such as maintenance (some stay for six months) and office work. The camp always needed help with copying, filing, and such.

Later, we were happy to learn that the camp offers a non-denominational church service at the beautiful chapel on the hill (really fun to bike to).

The YMCA Trout Lodge and Camp Lakewood are located on Sunnen Lake, just eight miles from Potosi, Missouri, and 90 minutes south of St. Louis in Missouri's Eastern Ozarks. If you'd like more information about the camp and its many opportunities, check out www.ymcaoftheozarks.org.

If you like new experiences, need exercise, like to meet new and interesting people, and are tired of cooking, we guarantee you'll love it there. (We just received an email from Amar from Egypt telling us he was home safe and was thinking about coming back next year.)

I hope you enjoyed hearing about our six weeks as workampers at the age of 71. We slept very well while we stayed there. Happy camping!

Tales of the Old Days

Janis Blake

We so envy the RVers of today. They have all the new technology that we sure could have used. Back in the '70s, GPS systems, cell phones, backup cameras to assist in backing up your vehicle, and satellite dishes were not available to us. We spent a lot of time asking for directions, turning around, and trying to find a gas station big enough to get into without backing up. I have many memories—some I'm not as fond of as others.

Our lives changed in 1974 when we sold everything and hit the road (something my husband, Dorian, had wanted to do for years). Little did we know what would come to be. For more than 28 years, we traveled the U.S. doing our "Magic and Illusion Show." We started out with just a van, staying in motels for the first year. (Motels were very reasonable in price then.)

After we moved into theatrical stage shows and the large Shrine Circus, we purchased our first trailer (21 feet). We towed it all over the U.S. until we outgrew it. We moved up to a 29-foot Wilderness in 1979. We loved that trailer. It seemed like we had the largest one at the shows we worked because everyone would end up at our place after the show or on a day off. We would all get together to eat, drink, and discuss what went right or wrong with the show. What fun.

Through the years, we've met lots of nice people and still stay in touch with many of them. Only true friends would help you change an axle in mud up to their knees, bring their elephant to pull you off a muddy circus lot, or drive you to the next town when you're suffering from food poisoning. Looking back, even the bad times were great.

Chapter 3

A Funny Thing Happened on the Way to . . .

Laughter is great for the soul. It's also great for your health. We need to laugh at ourselves and the funny, weird, and wacky things that happen along the road. We've all had experiences where "you just had to be there."

The goal of the following stories from our contributors is to put you "there." These tales from the road are sure to bring a smile to your face—and maybe you'll even say to yourself, hey, I really have been there!

The Marriage Penalty

Pete McMullen

One summer I found myself with a few extra days of vacation so I took our 34-foot motor home to a campground in southern Colorado where my wife was to join me that weekend. The campground will remain nameless as the RV sites left much to be desired. The leveling process involved about an hour of maneuvering the motor home on our assigned site to find the flattest spot. I used a combination of ramps and blocks before finally being able to extend the levelers. As I stood back to survey my success, a man with a small Class C motor home drove up, backed into an equally unleveled site, tossed out a lawn chair, and proceeded to open a beer. I called over to him, stating it had taken me an hour to park my RV. Why wasn't he even trying to level his? I will never forget his answer: "'Cause I ain't married."

The "BC"—A Mystery with a Humorous Outcome

A revered campground tale in the public domain

The story is told of a rather old-fashioned lady who was quite delicate and elegant, especially in language. She and her husband were planning a week's vacation in Florida, so she wrote to a campground office and asked for a reservation. She wanted to make sure the campground was fully equipped but didn't know how to ask about the toilet facilities because she just couldn't bring herself to write the word toilet in her letter. After much deliberation, she finally came up with bathroom commode, which she denoted merely as "BC."

"Does the campground have its own BC?" she wrote.

Well, the campground owner wasn't the old-fashioned prissy type at all. When he got this letter, he couldn't figure out what the woman was talking about. That "BC" business really stumped him. He showed the letter to several couples, but they couldn't imagine what the lady meant either. Finally concluding she must be asking about the location of the nearest Baptist Church, he wrote the following reply:

Dear Madam:

I regret the delay in answering your letter, but I now take the pleasure of informing you that a BC is located nine miles north of the campground and is capable of seating 250 people at one time. It is located in a beautiful pine grove and is open only on Sundays and Wednesdays. I admit it is quite a distance away if you are in the habit of going regularly, but no doubt you will be pleased to know that many people take their lunch along and make a day of it. They usually arrive early and stay late. My daughter met her husband in the BC. Sometimes it is so crowded, there are five to a seat. It may interest you to know that right now there is a supper planned to raise money to buy more seats. They are going to hold it in the basement of the BC. It pains me very much not to be able to go more regularly, but it is surely not due to a lack of desire on my part. As we grow older, it seems to be more of an effort, particularly in cold weather. If you decide to come to our campground, perhaps I could go with you the first time you go and sit with you and introduce you to all the other folks. We will be sure to get a seat up front where you can be seen by everyone. Remember, we are a friendly community.

Sincerely,

The Campground Owner

Will People Never Learn?

Anonymous

People watching can be great entertainment. Here's a great example: My wife and I watched a man trying to empty the holding tank of his RV. He filled a two-gallon bucket and then hauled it to a sewer pipe where he dumped it, sloshing the contents all over his pants and shoes as he walked. I tried to explain about a sewer hose, but clearly he knew better. After about 26 trips and much amusement on our part, he had finished the job. Maybe after a few aching backs, he will learn the benefits of using a hose.

Food Fiasco

Ernie Menold

We had rented our first motor home to travel to Disney World with our four teenagers. It was a 36-foot Winnebago. We were excited and busied ourselves packing and getting ready to go. My wife, Helen, was convinced that no food was sold south of the Mason-Dixon line so she cooked and fixed and jammed the refrigerator full. I think we had enough food for two trips.

Finally ready and eager for a great adventure, we pulled out of the driveway and got underway. Just 10 minutes from home, I made a left turn and suddenly heard a huge crash! Stunned, I stopped and looked around in time to see a huge bowl of potato salad sliding down the floor toward me. Following the potato salad was a shapeless blob of Jello, once well-formed in its Jello mold. After some serious laughter, we cleaned up the mess and got on the road again.

Catch Anything Yet?

Anita Henehan

One summer, we were campground hosts at Rocky Mountain National Park just outside Estes Park, Colorado. Our son, Paul, had paid to give his dad a day of fly fishing lessons. My husband, also Paul, had all the equipment he needed—the rod, the reel, the hip boots, and so on. He spent a whole day with a guide who took him to the west side of the Park, the lead headwaters of the Colorado River. This beautiful place was a perfect spot to learn to fly fish. Paul greatly enjoyed it.

The guide suggested Paul continue to practice casting, so he often went to a small lake near the campground where we were parked. One day as he was casting, the fish hook got caught on a tree behind him. He put on another hook and kept practicing. He did it again and lost yet another hook, so he continued casting without the hook. No wonder people walking kept asking him, "Catch anything yet?"

Chapter 4
Close Calls!

While we don't want to have those close calls—they still happen. It's those turns we almost didn't make, the things we came close to hitting, and those people on the road who are menaces (never us).

Be sure to travel safely and take warnings from these next stories.

A Rainy Night

Anita Henehan

We parked our coach at a campground near Gettysburg where we decided to stay for two nights. Weather reports warned to expect up to three inches of rain from Hurricane Isabel. The campground featured hookups in the middle of a huge field. Ordinarily, that would be fine, but with heavy rains expected, camping on a grassy field isn't the best idea.

We woke up in the morning to an overcast sky. As a precaution, before we went to Gettysburg for the day, we moved our coach to a pavilion where we could park on gravel. Thank goodness! That night, I was awakened by the torrential rains, and I started praying. All through the night, the winds and rain pelted and shook our 50,000-pound coach. My prayers were answered. By morning, the rains had subsided and the winds were much less fierce.

We continued on our journey to Lexington to see our family and thanked God for all our blessings.

A "Peaceful" Day at the Campground

Sue and John Mason

We decided to take our trailer and go to CoCo, Florida, to watch the NASCAR races. Our grandson, Cory, went with us. We were all excited because we love NASCAR. We chose the Sunrise Palms campground to park our trailer.

After angling our trailer into the campsite, we began relaxing for the day. Cory decided to move his lounge chair into the sun. At that moment, another travel trailer was backing into the site next to us and was coming in way too fast. The driver angled his trailer and hit the slide-out on the rig next to us, knocking it off its jacks before the trailer came to a stop. Thank God he was backing at an angle. John had grabbed Cory and pulled him out of the way fast or the driver might have hit our grandson. Unfortunately, the guy hit a brand new trailer. When he finally did stop, he sat there for about 20 minutes, apparently in shock. He evidently had pushed on the gas pedal instead of the brake.

Cory was eating a cookie when all this happened. In all the commotion and movement, the cookie flew into the air and under our RV. Cory's nonchalant response? "I don't think I'll eat that one."

An Unintended Almost Float Trip

Hilda Myers

As campground hosts, we had the job of assisting fellow campers every way we could. One cold night a terrible storm hit. The front section of the park had water and electric hookups while the back section offered primitive, or tent, camping.

Earlier that day, we'd checked in a few tent campers. One was a gentleman with his girlfriend.

As the rains came down, the Black River of Missouri rose. Soon it was flooding into the park. My husband, Curt, went out to warn the campers in tents, even evacuate them. Two campers were still left in the back area and we couldn't get through to them in our pickup truck during the flash flood.

All this time, the gentleman and his sweetie were inside their tent sound asleep on an air mattress. Another camper who was trapped on his site said he yelled many times to warn the couple but they didn't seem to hear him. As the water rose, first all the empty wine bottles came floating out of the tent, then the cooler. Then the whole tent, which wasn't tied down in any way, started floating back toward the river. The pair were still totally unaware of all of this as they continued to sleep on their floating bed. When the other camper realized the floating tent was being carried down into the river, he acted quickly, and after making it to the tent, woke up the couple and got them out of there. He surely saved their lives. I often wonder if the sleeping couple realized how close they'd come to becoming victims of the Black River flash flood.

This state park has since been totally destroyed by water and is being rebuilt. The incident certainly wasn't funny at the time, but since then, we've had a few good laughs about it.

A Blessing in Disguise

Anita Henehan

We had just left the Sun-N-Fun in Sarasota, Florida, after a delightful six weeks with new friends. We had a wonderful farewell picnic on Siesta Key beach that's white sand just like sugar. All our friends came to give us hugs and wave good-byes.

After being away so long, we were excited about going home, despite the long drive from Florida to Missouri. All was going well, or so we thought. We stopped at a Flying J for gas and after fueling up, we were driving on the ramp that would get us back on Hwy 75N. Unfortunately, our coach had trouble getting up this ramp. Knowing a 500 HP engine should not have trouble getting on or off any ramp, we stopped at a station down the road to see what the problem was. I kept praying, "Please, Lord and Angels, let this place be knowledgeable of coach motors." Paul added two quarts of transmission fluid and bought an extra quart for a spare. We were on the road again.

It may be said we're living the American Dream in our RV, which sounds good until problems hit. That day, we had to stop two more times to get fluid and add it to the transmission. Surely this would do the trick.

We decided to take Hwy 10 west to New Orleans and then Hwy 55 north to St. Louis because it's more level than going through the mountains. Even though the route via Hwy 10 is about 400 miles longer, it would be easier on the coach and we didn't want to tax the transmission. Well, we wouldn't get home as early, but we'd be safer.

When we stopped for lunch in Mississippi, Paul checked the transmission fluid—half empty—with a Flying J station still 30 miles away. What's worse, every time we would hit a bump, the transmission would shift gears. We arrived at the Flying J, fueled up, and asked to buy transmission fluid. None! Thankfully, a nice cashier directed us to Empire Truck Sales one exit east of the Flying J. There, Paul bought two cases of transmission fluid and added one case immediately, saving the other for later. We checked the fluid level several times as we traveled down the road. Luckily, the time changed to Central Time and we gained an hour as we traveled west.

Yet we were still "bumping" along the highway in Louisiana and it kept getting worse and worse, so we pulled over on Hwy 55 north and called AAA. After waiting two hours, AAA called back and said they couldn't find a tow truck that could pull our 42-foot coach weighing more than 50,000 pounds. So we decided we could make it to Jackson, Mississippi, on our own by traveling very slowly. It took us almost three hours to go 100 miles. Luckily, we found the roads in Mississippi better than in Louisiana, which made the ride much better. By the time we arrived at the place that could fix the coach, it was dark. As we drove into the driveway, the transmission light came on as well as the emergency light. We lost all power, but we'd reached our destination. Thank you, Lord and Angels!

That night was spent in the driveway of the repair shop. The next day, the technician there determined our problem was electrical, not the transmission at all. One of the battery cables for the coach was causing the trouble. The repair shop had to send to Jackson to get the right cable so we sat there for hours waiting for it. When it finally arrived, we discovered they'd sent the wrong cable. More waiting. Finally, the right cable arrived, it was installed, and everything started like clockwork. Hooray! Hooray! Thank you God, Angels, and Technicians.

What did we learn from this? When you're on the road, never be in a hurry.

Chapter 5
OOPS!

Stuff happens. We forget something, we fail to check on things, or we plan poorly. Sometimes even the most carefully laid plans hit a snag. It may not be a big one, but if you've been on the road for more than a week, you likely have had at least one "oops" moment, as these stories reveal.

Please Don't Pick the . . . Wildflowers

Jean Anderson

My husband and I work as interpreters for the United States Forest Service in the Big Horn National Forest of Wyoming. Our duty station is at Shell Falls Interpretive Center where we operate the Center and give interpretive talks to our visitors. Many of our talks are based on actual experiences with the people we meet there.

My favorite is a narrative about a five-year-old boy who entered the Center one day with a most determined air about him, as though he was on a mission. He walked directly to where I stood behind the counter and promptly began pulling on my pant leg. I looked down into his little face and he honored me with the most beautiful smile I had ever seen. As soon as he had melted me into a puddle of butter on the floor with that smile, up came one fist filled with wildflowers—as many as he could get his grubby little fingers around. And not just wildflowers, but Indian paintbrush—the Wyoming state flower. You're really not supposed to pick the Indian Paintbrush!

In the meantime, I noticed that a man had come into the room. I assumed (correctly) he was the little boy's father. Now, you have to understand I'd been working all day and I'd been serious about as long as I was going to be. It was time to have a little fun. Knowing that the father was listening, I walked over to the little boy and looked down at him. As he gave me another one of those wondrous smiles, I said, "You've got five, ten, fifteen . . . why you've got about four hundred dollars worth of illegal flowers there." The little guy just smiled; he didn't know the difference. But the father's face turned white. He could just see the rest of his vacation going up in wildflowers!

The little boy resumed pulling on my pant leg. Once again I looked down into that little face that still sported a smile, and he wiggled a tiny finger at me, asking me to lean over so he could whisper in my ear. I did just that and, raising his grubby little fist full of wildflowers, he said in a loud stage whisper, "These are for you." Can you imagine? I nearly had a stroke right there! He looked up at me and, with a child's intuition, could see something was wrong. So in an attempt to make it better, he added, "Oh no, don't worry about it. I've got a lot more of them out in the car."

The Dumped Dish

Anita Henehan

In a small RV park where we stayed in El Paso, Texas, the coaches were parked close together. As I chopped up a salad for lunch, I watched a man parked just a few spaces from us adjust his TV "dish." Every few minutes he came outside, made a few adjustments, gave himself a positive nod, and went back into the coach to check the reception. After a while, frowns replaced the nods. We were eating and he was still adjusting.

Finally, the dish was perfectly aligned. We never got to see the self-satisfied grin on his face as he was obviously enjoying his triumph inside. But just a few minutes later, a woman came down the row driving a little too fast. You guessed it; she knocked over the dish. The man ran outside looking both angry and defeated. Well, at least it wasn't broken. It was start-over time for him.

A Cold, Cold Shower—or Let This Be a Lesson

Darlene and Bill Heath

On a cold night at a desolate campground in Indiana, it was time for everyone to take a shower before going to bed. We were in our fold-down camper, which had no bathroom, so we trudged down the path to the campground's shower facilities—mom and the three sisters in one direction, dad and son in the other.

Usually the girls were last to return from the showers; however, this evening the girls were back and ready to go to bed when they heard their dad and brother moaning and laughing. They'd gone to the shower without any towels! And they didn't realize it until they stepped out of the water, cold and dripping wet. What could they do? They looked at each other and began to laugh. Even a magician couldn't produce a towel from nowhere! They tried drying off by swiping the water off with their hands while jumping around trying to get warm.

Of course, when they told the tale, the girls laughed hilariously, visualizing their dad and brother doing a warm-up dance. Yes, it was a cold, cold shower. And they've never forgotten a towel since.

Turn the Wheel Left—No, the Other Left!

Christine Budnik

Traveling the two-lane twisting road from Raleigh, North Carolina, to Pigeon Forge, Tennessee, certainly tested mind and limb on one trip. After battling the traffic in Gatlinburg, we finally arrived at the campground, where we were told our site was a pull-through. That would have been okay if we hadn't had large units sticking out on either side of us and the trees had been in more convenient places. We maneuvered around for about 10 minutes before returning to the office to ask for a different location.

After determining that no other suitable sites were available, the campground manager sent a young man to "help" us back in. We knew we were in trouble when he told my husband, David, to "Turn the wheel left—no, the other left!" After 45 minutes, during which we attracted quite a crowd and scraped our awning, we were finally parked. We put the jacks down and unhooked the electricity and brake cables.

Tired and frustrated, as I turned away I thought, "There's no reason for the tailgate to be down anymore." You guessed it. I closed it. Then my husband put the truck in drive. He stopped when he heard the crunch of the hitch hitting the tailgate.

Bless him! David reminded me that he has also done "stupid" things and said that if this was our worst disaster, we could count ourselves fortunate. Just another adventure.

Unexpected Dip

Darlene Heath

On our way from Indiana to the Calgary Stampede in Calgary, Canada, we stopped for the night in Minot, North Dakota. We picked a nice campsite with a pretty view beside a small bayou. The sun had just begun to set, and as we were doing the usual setup chores, we noticed a limb was caught in the television antenna on top of our RV. My husband, Bill, stayed outside to remove it while I went inside.

I was concentrating on leveling the RV and extending the slide-outs, when I heard a knock on the door. When I opened it, there stood Bill dripping wet! He had tried repeatedly from the ground to dislodge the limb. It wouldn't budge. So finally he climbed the ladder to the top of the RV. Bad decision! As he was descending the ladder, his foot slipped and into the bayou he fell! The sloping bank was covered with weeds and mud—and so was he. Picture a half man, half bayou creature. His shoes were oozing mud with weeds "growing" out of them! His billfold was so soaked we had to use the microwave to dry it.

Periodic shoulder pains from the fall are a reminder of his plunge into the bayou. We laugh every time we recall the scene, and we're grateful he was able to drag himself out of the water. Otherwise, he could have disappeared without a trace. It turned out to be just an unexpected dip.

Remember the Laws of Physics

Curt and Hilda Myers

A camper carefully backed his travel trailer into a sloping hillside campsite, then proceeded to level it on a set of 45-degree wheel chocks. After he thought it was level, he unhooked it from his tow vehicle. The laws of physics took over from that point, and just like Jack and Jill, the trailer came tumbling down the hill. Thankfully, no casualties were incurred.

Busted!

Rhonda and Ken Hardy

Across from our site at Sun-N-Fun RV resort in Sarasota, Florida, we watched a young couple and their dog, Penelope, move in.

We immediately fell in love with Penelope, a bearded collie and duplicate of the dog in the movie The Shaggy Dog. After Penelope's "mom," Rhonda, adopted the dog, she attended an event near their home called "Bark in the Park." There were 5,000 dogs at the event. At one of the stations, a sign said they trained dogs to assist in therapy service. Rhonda signed up Penelope. The animals are trained to go to nursing homes and hospice situations as well as juvenile centers. She thought Penelope would be best in nursing homes where people could pet her and feel her love.

Who knew that this gentle dog would be "busted" by the Sun-N-Fun RV Park "Nazi" who makes rounds and checks to see if any dog is on a leash longer than eight feet. This "Nazi" busted Penelope because her leash was a little longer than the limit. It was so funny to think that this placid dog—the one who never barks and just licks you to pieces—got busted.

Oh well. Rules are rules wherever you go.

Some People Never Learn

Curt and Hilda Myers

Volunteering as a campground host has its funny side. In the state park where we hosted, campers have to leave at the end of the weekend. One of the campers was a little harried and running late. He had been hooking up his fifth-wheel trailer. To hook up this type of trailer, a kingpin is inserted into a receiver hitch in the center of the truck bed and locked. He thought he was all hooked up and ready to go, but as he pulled out of his site, everyone could hear a loud BANG! The trailer landed on the sides of his pickup bed, putting a nice deep V in the side walls of the truck. He had forgotten to lock the receiver. People rushed forward to assist, but his only comment was, "No thanks, I can handle this. I've done it before."

Don't Pull that Lever!

Curt and Hilda Myers

One of our favorite stories as volunteer camp hosts is about the couple who had bought themselves a brand new motor home. They were mighty proud of it. The wife decided to do the grand tour for some friends and proceeded to show everyone how every little gadget worked, inside and outside. All was going well until she arrived at the lower back of the trailer and was explaining the sewer mechanism. In her zeal, she reached up and pulled the release lever on the sewer tank. As you can imagine, out came several days of sewage right in her face! She wiped herself off and said, "At least I know it's ours!"

Lost Little Girl

Darlene and Bill Heath

One night, our 2½-year-old daughter disappeared. We had just seen her outside our RV. We questioned our other three children but they just shook their heads. Then suddenly, one of them remembered seeing her go inside the camper. We looked in but didn't see her. Then we heard a faint rattling sound coming from the direction of the bathroom. Soon those sounds changed to a small voice whimpering. "I can't get out of here!" it said.

She had gone into the bathroom, locked the door, and couldn't get it unlocked! Each of us, eager to ease her panic, was giving her instructions at the same time. What chaos! Still unable to unlock the door, she was scared and began to cry, thinking she was stuck in there forever!

Have you ever tried to remove the bathroom door from inside the confines of a camper? Well, that was the only apparent solution. We quickly gathered the right tools while trying to calm our increasingly frantic daughter. Finally the door was off and out came a half-smiling little girl with arms outstretched and tears still streaming down her cheeks. We all cheered for the not-so-lost little girl.

Thanks a Lot, John!

Maggie MacFarlane

Traveling down the road at a pretty fast clip, we rounded a corner and a tractor trailer came alongside us carrying a wide load. The tractor trailer moved closer to the guardrail, and we moved, too. Suddenly an iron bar about two feet long flew out of the wide load and smashed our rearview mirror to bits.

I wanted to stop, but John, my husband, said we needed to wait until we got to a wide place in the road. Finally, we found a safe spot to pull the coach over. John jumped out to inspect the damage. I had to get out of the coach, too. Mrs. McNosey, as John calls me, hit the red button on the door as she was getting out of the coach and locked the door. John cursed a blue streak.

Picture this, if you can. We're on a major road, Route 80. We have three animals inside the coach—one dog weighing 185 pounds plus a little cocker spaniel and a cat. The coach is locked and the motor is running. Okay, what do we do now?

John got the ladder and put it next to the driver's side where the window was open. I climbed up attempting to get into the coach through the window. John put his hands on my rear end to help boost me up higher. I finally managed to reach the keys, which I handed back to John. He proceeded to take the ladder away, leaving me hanging half in the coach and half out, my legs waving in the wind. I was stuck, and he never came to help me! Finally, I was able to wiggle the rest of the way through the window and slip into the driver's seat, safe at last! As you can imagine, the tractor trailer drivers were honking as they drove by—and tons of them take Route 80. Talk about embarrassed. Thanks a lot, John!!

Nearly Lost Teeth

Marianne Cavanaugh

We were camping at Silver River in Ocala National Forest. The site had electric and water only, with no place to dump sewage. Our tank was close to full, and we were trying to conserve on water so Joe, my husband, wouldn't have to dump it.

When it came time to brush his teeth, Joe took out the partial he wore and put it in a bowl of water. After brushing his teeth, he tossed the water outside. Whoops! Out went the partial. I had gone for a walk, and when I returned, we spent several hours looking for the silvery partial, which blended in with the silver sand.

We didn't find it and actually thought a squirrel had taken it. We even tried to find it using our high-powered binoculars. Finally we gave up and returned to the coach. The only thing to do was look on the Internet for a place that makes partials.

Joe was so upset. He had been planning to go to seminars and meet lots of people. How could he talk to them without his teeth? A toothless grin wasn't too appealing. How embarrassing! But instead of lamenting, we decided to laugh about the situation. What else could we do?

Later I went out for another look—and guess what. There was Joe's partial. I went back to the coach with a grin on my face, the hero of the day.

Don't Forget Your Wife

Jeannine Robbins

On May 24th (our son's birthday), I had just showered and, because it was hot, I was wearing my romper with the elastic top and shorts attached. We left our KOA campsite but missed the entrance to Highway 40W. Nevertheless, we continued down the road toward the nearest town. As we drove, the black rubber water cover came off our RV. My husband, Fentar, stopped the coach to recover it. I got out on my side and Fentar got out on his side. When he got the cover back on, Fentar climbed back in the coach and started driving. He didn't know I never got back in!

I tried to flag my husband down, but he didn't see me waving furiously. As luck would have it, I saw a state trooper. I waved at him, but at first he thought I was just being friendly. I shouted, "Please stop, I need you!" He pulled over and I told him what had just happened. So the trooper drove on to find Fentar, who, as it turned out, was talking to me—but of course I wasn't there. He told me (he thought), "We're being pulled over, but I don't know why."

He said to the trooper, "Good morning." The trooper responded, "Good morning, sir. Do you know you left your wife in Halbrook?" Shocked, Fentar replied, "I've heard of this happening before, but I never thought it would happen to me."

That evening we called our son, Dennis, to wish him a happy birthday and told him what had happened. Fentar quipped, "I was talking to Jeannine and she didn't answer me. Oh, well, your mother never answers me anyway."

Chapter 6

Friends Along the Way

One of the greatest treats of RV travel is meeting new friends along the way. People from all backgrounds enjoy the road. It's as though we belong to a special club and we've pledged to help each other.

I have learned and laughed and celebrated lots as I've traveled throughout North America. I cherish my new friends. Some I meet only once; others become lifelong friends. And each brings a new gift of experience and adventure.

A Royal Welcome

Anita Henehan

We learned that friends we'd arranged to meet for the second year at the Sun-N-Fun RV Park in Sarasota, Florida, were experiencing health issues. Doctors had told Sue that, due to some medical problems, she might have to have an operation. All of us RVers who knew Sue and Norm were greatly concerned. When she was finally cleared to travel, we were thrilled that they would still come to Florida for the winter. Although they were leaving a few days later than planned, we learned they'd soon be on the road again.

A few days later, we got news that the traveling couple had not only blown two tires but also had a hole in the rig. They continued to have problems with their coach, including radiator replacement and transmission problems. Enough already! Then they had to stay in a motel for several days after the coach had to be towed more than 200 miles to get repaired. Their saga continued like a bad novel.

Every day someone from our RV Park talked to Norm to find out their status. He told us they had to empty the coach of all their food, giving away what they had in the refrigerator to homeless people. Finally, we got word they were really on the road to Sarasota. Everyone wanted to give them a special welcome so we went to Target and bought poster board, paints, brushes, and white wrapping paper and fashioned a giant "finish line." Some of the talented artists turned the posters into drawings of Margaritaville with palm trees and a man relaxing underneath. How cute. Another sign stated the repair prices for new tires, new radiator, and new transmission. We stood two of the picnic tables on end to hold the "finish line" roll of paper. One neighbor, Sam, had a margarita machine and kept the drinks coming. The tables were adorned with umbrellas as the music played Jimmy Buffet's Margaritaville. What a scene as Sue and Norm rolled in!

You see, we all really care about these guys. That day, they felt the love we have for them. We partied all afternoon and into the evening. What a BLAST to be remembered forever.

Answered Prayers

Wayne Cox

My wife, Betty, and I had just driven our motor home, towing a Ranger pickup truck, all the way from Indianapolis to Tampa, Florida. I drove so perfectly that not a single driver blasted a horn at us.

Actually I can't take credit for my good driving. Betty is so nervous about RV travel that before we enter each highway, she takes my hand and listens as I say this prayer:

I thank God for providing us with this late model motor home in good mechanical condition;

I ask that He provide me with the alertness and skills needed to drive safely;

I also ask He provide the same alertness and skills to the drivers around us;

I thank Him for this beautiful world He has created for us to visit and enjoy;

I ask in the name of Jesus that the Father be with us throughout the day to advise us as we travel and to keep us from harm's way.

As I end the prayer with Amen, Betty moves the road atlas from the dash to her lap. She places the point of her pen directly on our exact location and begins to draw a "highlighted highway" on the map she'd prepared the night before. Here's the dialogue that typically follows:

"Is the parking brake off?" she asks.

"Turn right, go two blocks, then turn left."

"Move to the left lane—now!" she commands.

"Watch out for the little red car."

"You're going too fast—S L O W down!!"

"Watch the green light ahead—slow down, I think it's about to turn red—get ready for the brakes."

"Boy, were we lucky on that one."

"Watch it, watch it, don't get too close to the edge—it's a deep drop-off."

"I don't care if the sign does say you can drive 70 miles an hour; we agreed not to drive over 60."

"Man, did you see that?"

"The mirror on that semi that just passed us missed my mirror by only a couple of inches; move to the right lane so they can't pass on my side anymore."

"You're too close to the car in front of us; back off."

"Don't forget, we don't have to be in a hurry to get anyplace. If we don't get there today, we can make it tomorrow—okay?"

"Okay," I say.

"No, I do not want to stop at the rest park up ahead," she replies. "It's too dangerous getting this long rig back into traffic. I don't understand how you know where our pickup is when we cut

into traffic; you can't see it in the mirrors. I worry we're going to slap a little car into the ditch."

"Slow down! You're going so fast I can't read the exit numbers!"

"It's three-thirty and we've been on the road for six hours. I have a nice little RV park picked out for tonight. Slow down. Turn off at the next exit—no, not this exit, the next exit. Wait until I tell you to turn off, okay?"

"Okay," I reply.

"Exit the interstate now. Turn right, go one mile then turn left on County Road 400, go 3.4 miles, the RV park will be on the right," she instructs. "When you register, don't forget to ask for a pull-through site, so we don't have to back in."

I remind her, "We don't need a pull-through. I'm very good at backing this motor home into a tight spot."

"I know you are, dear," she answers, "but I like pull-through sites, so ask for a pull-through, okay?"

"Okay," I reply again.

Dear friends, you've just experienced a typical day with Betty and Wayne traveling in their RV—an experience like no other. After being on the road 72 days in 1999 and more in years that followed, you must admit, we're experienced RVers. But I still find it amazing that not one time have I allowed the motor home to drop off the edge of the road, nor have we had a close call of any type. And only twice have drivers sounded their horns to express dismay with my driving.

Is it because I am such a perfect driver? I think not. I think it's God answering my prayer requesting He give me the alertness and skills needed to drive the motor home safely. The way I see it, being aware of my natural alertness and driving skills, God has determined I need close supervision. I have concluded that on each trip when I finish my prayer, Amen becomes the cue for the Holy Spirit to climb aboard our motor home and ride with us all day. He takes a position so he can whisper God's driving instructions into Betty's ear. She repeats God's words, adds a few of her own, and as a result, my prayer request for a safe and enjoyable trip is answered. At times, God seems to work in unusual and mysterious ways; however, I am convinced He always answers our prayers.

Angels on the Road

Karan Johnson

We were off to Lazy Daze to use a three-day pass. Lazy Daze is an RV dealer in Tampa, Florida, that's also an RV park where you can stay for a few days at no charge. We started having trouble with the truck but didn't listen to the technician we consulted and neglected to change the fuel filter. He'd quoted a price of $48, and Herman, my husband, thought that was too pricey. After all, he knew he could do it himself. As we traveled on to Cypress Gardens, Savannah, Georgia, I had it in my mind that we needed to change the fuel filter, but we were having so much fun we completely forgot about it. We continued to the Smokey Mountains, and when we got into Canton, North Carolina, the truck started jerking in the mountains. I knew something was wrong.

We pulled off the highway, and the truck started running better. Problem solved. But back on the highway, the truck quit running after a few miles. The first miracle was that we managed to find a wide spot where we could pull off easily. Herman started investigating and deemed it was the filter. He tried to drain the fuel filter and dropped the drain plug. It disappeared. He started panicking. After all, it was Sunday. Where would we get help and find the part we needed? He backed up the truck and still couldn't locate the plug. He spent an hour taking off the inner fender well, getting more rattled by the minute.

We looked up to see a state trooper. He had just appeared out of nowhere!

"Are you okay?" he inquired. "We're fine," replied Herman. Why do we always give that standard answer? We weren't fine. The trooper gave us his cell number in case we wanted his help. Herman called AAA for roadside service and learned someone would arrive within four hours. Clearly, we were stuck.

This was Herman's first mechanical failure. He'd always been able to fix all our vehicles—trucks, boats, coach. This time, he gave up. I was scared we'd be mugged if we had to stay overnight.

Enter the angels. Charles and Darlene stopped and asked if they could be of assistance. (They were RVers from Canton, North Carolina.) Charles was sure the fuel filter was plugged. He offered that if we couldn't get help, he and Herman could get a fifth-wheel hitch at their house to tow the vehicle. But he said, "Let's try one more time."

We managed to get the truck started and barely made it to Walmart 10 miles down the road. Charles called a supplier that was still open. They bought the right fuel filter and Charles installed it. Herman was still shaken by the ordeal. Charles and Darlene said they would follow us 100 miles and if we broke down, we could call them.

We're so thankful that when Charles and Darlene saw us off the road, they turned around to help. They were truly our angels who demonstrated how the world should be—people helping people.

Another Stroke of Luck

Anita Henehan

We were in Alaska having a grand old time. Everything was going along very well, or so we thought. Just 20 miles outside of Anchorage, we heard a POP. Yes, a flat tire. As luck would have it, my handy dandy husband was in the process of changing the tire when a kind man stopped to help him. "Everyone helps each other," he said. What a wonderful way of life.

Making New Friends

Hilda Myers

There we were, on our first assignment as volunteer camp hosts in a state park in Missouri and green as grass. My husband, Curt, was making rounds in the park and came upon a camper lying in a hammock strung between two trees. It was against the rules to string a hammock between trees, as the camper must have known. He said, "I bet you're going to tell me to take down the hammock." He seemed to be prepared for Curt's response.

As my husband was leaving the site, the camper asked, "Do you like pork steak?" When Curt said yes, we were invited to dinner. That was the beginning of a friendship with Dale and Maryanne that has continued for the last 15 years.

Never Give Up

Roslyn Schickel

We were driving south from Pennsylvania, trying to outrun a storm in North Carolina. The weather wasn't the best. We'd driven way too many hours and were exhausted. Finally, at ten o'clock, we stopped for the night.

The next day, we arrived at Tarpon Springs. My husband, Stewart, must have strained his eyes as he was having trouble backing into the RV spot. At the dinner table, he admitted, "I can only see half of you." We knew we needed to see an eye specialist.

Someone parked next to us gave us the name of an ophthalmologist who, luckily, had an office only a few blocks away. The doctor diagnosed Stewart's condition as a "detached retina." Stewart ended up having three surgeries while we stayed in Tarpon Springs. After the operations, he had to sit in a chair with his head on a pillow and was allowed to move his head for only 10 minutes every hour.

People we were parked next to brought us food and checked on us regularly. Our whole family was worried. Our son-in-law was even prepared to take off work.

We had reservations in Fort Meyers Beach so we needed to move on. The man parked behind us, a total stranger, offered to drive our truck pulling our 28-foot trailer. His wife would follow behind to bring him back. I declined his incredibly kind offer and bravely decided I would drive our trailer myself.

A neighbor helped us hook up. Behind the wheel, I was scared to death at first. Ft. Meyers Beach was about 200 miles away. Traffic was horrendous.

But that wasn't the end of it. I had to drive back to Tarpon Springs for Stewart's checkups, and then I drove 1,000 miles home to Trafford, Pennsylvania. I proved that women can do anything when they're challenged!

Stewart had to have three more operations on his eye after we got home. He wanted to sell the truck that pulled the fifth-wheel trailer, but I emphatically disagreed. We decided we were too young to quit traveling. In fact, we proceeded to buy a bigger fifth wheel and have been traveling ever since. I still do the driving. We were determined to continue living life to the fullest despite the challenges.

The most amazing thing about this experience is that total strangers were so willing to help with whatever we needed. We are still in total awe of RVers' commitment to help others.

Chapter 7
Trouble on the Road

This is the part none of us like. But it happens. Things break or don't work. The weather turns nasty, the map is wrong, or the repair shop is closed the day you need it.

If these things happen to you, you aren't alone. You might even smile a bit as you read the next stories from RV friends.

Badlands and Bungee Cords

Ken and Janet Frey

In September, 2005, we traveled from our home in southeastern Pennsylvania to South Dakota for a GMC Motor Home International Rally. It was not a leisurely drive because we both still worked full time and couldn't take many days off. We were traveling 10 or 11 hours a day.

Our 1976 GMC Palm Beach motor home purred along. Of course, we stopped at lots of gas stations, but we also found charming local restaurants and stayed overnight in a few Walmart parking lots. When we arrived in eastern South Dakota, we thought, "Finally!" But actually, our destination was Rapid City—in western South Dakota. Five hundred miles to go!

Heading west, strong southerly winds pushed against the side of the motor home. Our mileage dropped drastically as the motor home fought against the force trying to push it off the road. Passing motorcycles leaned at crazy angles just to keep traveling straight. Then the wind actually reached under the driver's side awning and pulled it open! In 17 years, this had never happened before. The awning is approximately 18 feet long and about three feet wide when open. The spring tension system normally keeps the awning closed when not in use. But the wind was powerful enough to overcome this spring tension and keep the awning open until we slowed down. Then the awning slammed closed. This event was repeated several times.

Concerned that a passing truck would damage the awning or that it could cause an accident, we decided to stop and try to increase the tension of the spring. Confident that we had solved the problem, we returned to the highway and continued west. But soon we heard that familiar sound of the awning opening and slamming shut. We needed a different solution, so we stopped to ponder our next move. Ah—the old reliable bungee cord! Several cords going across the roof to the awning on the other side did the trick. This arrangement remained in place until we returned to Pennsylvania five days later.

Later, at a tourist center, we discovered that these high winds are not unusual out there. In fact, the owner of a campground in Kennebec, South Dakota, mentioned that many visitors stopped in with awnings severely damaged or totally ripped off. We were lucky!

By the way, we did get to Rapid City, had a great time at the rally, and were totally awed by Mount Rushmore and the Badlands. The trip was definitely worthwhile!

The Coach from Hell

Ernie Menold

My wife, Helen, and I bought a brand new motor coach right off the lot. Needless to say, we were excited. However, when we started driving it, we found it had no headlights, only running lights. This meant we could drive it only in the daytime. We wanted to call the salesman and get our money back. We discovered this (first!) problem as we were traveling through Virginia. We had to pull off the road until something was done. The dealer allowed us to get the headlights repaired.

When we got back to the campground, we found we had no heat. Luckily, we had an electric heater. We had to use a crock pot for dinner, and thankfully, we had a coffee pot. Back to the place that had repaired the lights.

We wanted to watch TV, but neither the satellite nor the cable connection was working.

We thought everything was fixed, but not so. What else could go wrong? We heard a loud POP then SWISH. Water was pouring out from under the refrigerator. We used every towel we had to mop it up. Somehow we found the shutoff valve to stop the water.

Again, back to the coach repair shop.

Was our coach ever going to be totally fixed? We wondered whether we should just give it back to the dealer.

In the end, we decided to get all the repairs taken care of. So far, all is well.

Snowy Valentine

June Garrison

Few people would dare take a 300-mile trip in a blizzard in a rented RV with seven kids and an 80-year-old father to celebrate Valentine's Day—but we did.

I called a friend who owned several RVs to reserve one for our Valentine's Day weekend. He had only one available. I reserved it for Friday, February 12th. Luckily, it slept six people, which was perfect. It had enough space for my grandchildren and my father could sit up front with me.

I picked up the RV and, by 8:30 in the evening, I'd packed everything we would need for our six-hour trip. Plenty of blankets, snacks for munching, and because I had no small containers, my five gallons of bottled water. By 9:00, I was in bed. My alarm was set for 4:30 a.m. I'd called everyone and told them to be packed and ready at our designated time Saturday morning.

My plan was in place. I would make three stops to pick up my passengers and, I hoped, be on Route 23 North by six, heading for my son Doug's house in Cedar, Michigan.

The first stop would be in Perrysburg, just seven blocks from my home. Destiny, my 15-year-old granddaughter and her best friend, Jaimie, were to be ready and waiting at 4:50 a.m. My second stop would be 16 miles north in Toledo, where I'd pick up my father and my grandson Gabriel, aka "The Gabe." He's the child who's six going on 11—clever and unpredictable. We were to be there by 5:15 a.m. My third and last stop would be 20 miles north in Allen's Cove, Michigan, on a narrow one-lane road along the shoreline of Lake Erie. There I'd pick up my two nine-year-old granddaughters, Amber and Angelica, eight-year-old Tristan, and seven-year-old Justin.

Friday's weather forecast for Saturday was snow, some flurries, with temperatures dropping into the low 30s. Our schedule on Saturday was perfect. All went well. Everyone was up and dressed, waiting to be picked up. However, the weatherman's forecast was a bit off. The "snow flurries" were becoming more of snowstorm, and the farther north we drove, the worse the conditions became.

Jerry, the RV owner, must have overlooked checking the windshield wiper blades because they were not doing a good job of keeping the freezing snow off. To make matters worse, the RV would only go 50 miles an hour max. The slush from the other cars, especially the semis, made the situation worse.

The children fell asleep. My father was sleeping, too, and I had to lean forward to see the road. The windshields were streaked with wet snow, and the headlights must have been covered with frozen slush. I was looking for a road sign that would tell me where to cross from I-75 North to I-23 North. I had no clue where we were. I figured the best thing would be to turn off onto the next side road to the west. I found one, hoping it would take us to I-23. Not so! It was a country road with ditches on both sides. I prayed I'd find a service station. I kept mumbling to myself, "I'm alone and I'm lost."

Just as I began to think I was staying in control of my situation, I saw one of the children coming to the front of the RV. Oh no! It was the Gabe. He leaned over and whispered in my ear, "Nanna, my belly hurts and I feel like I have to throw up." Stay cool, don't panic, I told myself.

"Gabe, go back to the restroom and do whatever you have to do," I said to him.

About that time Amber woke up. I motioned for her to help Gabe. Two minutes later, she came up behind me and whispered, "Nanna, the toilet doesn't flush. We don't have water." Suddenly it occurred to me. RVs don't have water in the winter because it freezes. DUH!

The best thing I could think of to tell Amber was to get two plastic garbage bags from under the sink. Put one down in the toilet and put one on Gabe's cap in case he gets sick. If we ever find a service station, I thought, we can throw it all into a trash receptacle. I trusted Amber to help the Gabe.

I was still trying to see out the windshield and not slip off into one of the ditches while still praying for a service station. By now, Gabe had gone back to bed, naked and smelling awful. Everyone in the back threatened to throw Gabe off the RV. Mutiny! What do I do? I can't stop, but I also can't keep driving!

Suddenly, my prayers were answered. I could see a white building just ahead—a church with a parking lot. Thank you, Lord! It took at least 45 minutes to clean up the mess and wash the Gabe (using my five-gallon water supply). But he was naked, and his other clothes were in the storage area in the back of the RV. The only thing to do was to get out in the snowstorm and wade through the slush to the back of the RV. I prayed that the doors to the storage area weren't frozen shut. No luck. They were. By this time everyone was awake and no one was happy. My father came back with a screwdriver and chipped away at the snow and ice until he popped open one of the doors. Even though

I didn't have a flashlight handy, I managed to feel around among all the luggage and found the Gabe's bag. Lucky for me he'd packed his things in a pillow slip. Dad and I closed the back doors, making sure they locked. We didn't want everyone else's luggage to fall out on the highway.

Alas, when we checked Gabe's pillowcase, he'd packed no clothes! We managed to dress him in Angelica's grey sweatpants, my father's red sweatshirt, and Justin's boots. No underwear. All of the borrowed clothing was three to five sizes too big. But what else could we do?

After everything was cleaned and all the icky stuff hermetically sealed in black plastic trash bags, the crew settled down. Dad scraped the windows clean, and we continued down the road. We began to see lights ahead. A service station was just opening for business. Although it was small with only two pumps, a fresh pot of coffee was brewing. It felt like an oasis! We pulled in and took our black plastic, hermetically sealed garbage bags and dropped them in the dumpster. Dad and I each bought big cups of fresh coffee, and the owner, a farmer, gave us directions to I-23. It was just three miles up the road.

The roads were still covered with snow and ice. The snow had subsided, and the sun would be coming up in less than a half hour. As we made a right turn onto I-23, the sun appeared on the horizon. The snow ceased to fall, and the three-lane highway had been plowed and salted.

I took a deep breath and relaxed for the first time in the last two hours. I loosened my grip on the steering wheel and pushed back the seat. Glancing up, I looked into the rearview mirror at the kids in the top bunk hanging upside down and having a pillow fight with the kids on the bottom bunk. My dad must have seen the look on my face because he smiled and said, "Do we know how lucky we are?"

I answered his question. "You know what, Dad? I don't care if this trip costs five hundred dollars. It's worth it to spend a day and a half with Doug and Myles, skiing and sledding and walking on the sandy beaches finding heart-shaped rocks and seeing those kids back there having a good time."

Dad smiled again and with teary eyes said, "Some things can't be bought with money, and this is one of those things. We're so lucky, aren't we?"

Patience is the Name of the Game

Sue Goulet

We left Nashua at five in the morning with the temperature minus five degrees. We were traveling from New Hampshire to Sarasota, Florida. About four miles down the highway the motor started acting up something terrible. "What the heck is that?" we wondered. We got off the highway and into a parking lot to check things out. Our left directional signal wasn't working even though it had been working when we left home. Then the brake light came on and wouldn't shut off. Then our Traction ATC light came on and stayed on. At minus five degrees, you can imagine what shape we were in mentally. We turned the RV around and went to Camper's Inn, knowing we couldn't drive the RV in that shape.

I am not a morning person to begin with, so you can imagine the "great" mood we were both in. Plus, I think I got frostbite on my toes. At least it felt like it.

A man at Camper's Inn said they would check out our RV, guessing the left blinker malfunction was caused by a broken line and it shouldn't take long to repair. Most likely the other problems were caused by the frigid weather. Great! So we waited, and finally Norm told me to take the car home and he'd wait there with the rig. He would pick me up.

No sooner did I get home than the phone rang, Norm telling me to pick him up at Camper's Inn because it looked like it would take all day to fix the problems. Here it was 11:00 and we hadn't yet left home! It seems we never go anywhere without an adventure. Norm hinted that I should fly to Florida and meet him there. What, no adventure?

Day two, we picked up our RV at the dealership to leave for Florida. Luckily, the dealer had plugged it in so we would have heat. It had warmed up only one degree to minus six. We were excited to finally be on our way! We got the Explorer hooked up to the RV and started to pull out of the parking lot when I suggested we double check the directional signal on the Explorer. I jumped out to see. Oops! No directional signal on the car.

Help!!! Please God, we've had enough. We played around with the connections for about an hour. By then, I could no longer feel my toes or fingers. There was nothing left to do but park the RV and go out to breakfast . . . again. When the RV dealer opened at 8 a.m., we pulled the car in and got the plug that connects to the motor home repaired. Finally, we were on our way—only 36 hours late getting started. Patience is the name of this game.

Burning Brakes

Anita Henehan

As we left Muncho Lake, British Columbia, about 9:30 in the morning, Paul smelled something burning in the brakes. Big Red, our Chevy Tahoe, had been doing a terrific job of pulling Merrily We Roll Along, our 25-foot trailer. But apparently it was "burning out." We decided to drive to Fort Nelson to see if we could get the car fixed. We were told to try the Chevy dealer in Fort St. John. So after driving 350 miles, we arrived there pooped! We hoped they could fix the car by the next day.

We got up early and found out the guy at the Chevy dealer couldn't fix the car until the following week. Plan B: We called ahead to Dawson Creek. They said they might be able to fix it that day or the next for sure. So off we went to Dawson Creek, an hour's drive away.

There, we stayed at Tubby's RV Park, conveniently located just one and a half blocks east of the Alaska/Hart junction, at mile zero where the Alaska Highway begins. The sites are level with easy entries and pull-throughs. The park has a car and RV wash, and it's close to a swimming pool, pioneer village, and restaurants. Plus, it's next to Dawson Creek Golf Course. All these amenities make Tubby's a choice RV park. (Phone: 250-782-2584)

We took the car in about 3:30 that day, hoping it would be ready the next morning. We also prayed the work would be under warranty. Paul cleaned the trailer and I washed clothes. What a team. After chores, we walked from the car dealer to the Alaska Café and Hotel and ate a delicious meal, then enjoyed the mile-or-so walk back to the campground.

Ah, synchronicity! The people we were camped next to in Seward pulled alongside us at Tubby's. They had experienced car trouble themselves and had waited three days to get a new clutch installed in their truck. But everyone helped them as they have us. I always so appreciate how people help each other "on the road." We picked up the car the next morning at the Chevy dealer. It was fixed and everything was under warranty. We were so lucky! Back on the road for another adventure and more new friends.

Pet Peeve

Anonymous

We all have pet peeves, don't we? One that tops my list is when campgrounds charge extra for tiny cats and dogs. Our well-behaved (cough, cough) Shitzu weighs in at approximately 10 pounds.

When I explained my concern to an RV park manager, he replied with this: "They drink the water." My retort: "The dog drinks what I drink, and it's out of a bottle." His comeback: "Pay or leave." We paid.

Tip: If you're an RVer with a dog, you might want to get the book in the Woodall's series of campground directories titled *Camping and RVing with Dogs.* (See Things That Are Good to Know at the end of the book.)

Praying Does Help

Anita Henehan

On a trip out east, we drove into Pennsylvania from New York and managed to find a campground after dark. We will never leave it that late again!

We parked the coach and plugged into the electric, but found out the water had been turned off for the season. We were about to fix dinner when suddenly everything shut down—lights, water, everything! If you don't have electricity to pump the water, you have no water.

Paul, the mechanic and coach driver, was stumped. He tried every possibility he knew to get the power to work. We had a generator, but even that didn't get the system going. We had no heat, and we had no water pump, which meant no toilet, no shower, no washing hands, no washing dishes. Okay what do we do now?

We got out the manual. We called Bruce, the technician at Ledford's where we'd bought the coach. Luckily, we had his home number, but unluckily, he wasn't home, so we called Bob, the salesman at Ledford's. He wasn't home either. Now what?

It was time for me to pray. Paul was beside himself. He can usually fix these things. We prepared to go to bed with all our clothes on and hoped the problem would correct itself in the morning. I was praying Big Time by now . . . and kept calling Bruce, hoping he would get home soon.

In the meantime, it was getting colder in the coach. Paul decided to try turn the power on once more. He started the coach and put it in gear. A miracle!! The lights came on. Water, heat—hooray!! I really believe it was the prayers that did it. Who knows, who cares? We were so grateful!!! We did some deep breathing, gave a sigh of relief, then took our showers and had a good night's sleep.

The next day when we finally got in touch with Bruce, he said we might have a solenoid (metal coil—long story) going bad—something that would cause all the systems to shut down. Even the generator wouldn't help. Whatever it was, we were rolling again. Thank you, Lord!

Tip: Stop and find a place to stay BD (Before Dark). No matter how eager you are to make road time, it's not worth the AD (After Dark) stress.

Pick out a possible destination according to approximately how far you want to travel for the day. Be sure to plan to arrive Way Before Dark (WBD). Pick your preferred RV park and call to see if it's open and available. A cell phone, although aggravating at times, comes in handy.

When you arrive at a reasonable hour, you can get set up, take a walk, and relax before dinner. And if a problem arises, it's always easier to fix before nightfall.

The Hail Storm We'll Never Forget

Anita Henehan

Heading for Colorado from St. Louis, we spent our first night in Abilene, Kansas. It's a lovely quiet town to visit. However, both Kansas and Colorado have a reputation for hail storms. We sometimes have them in our home town of St. Louis, too. As we drove, the clouds began to darken. I mean really darken. Hanging low overhead was the biggest, meanest looking cloud I'd ever seen. I felt that if I reached up, I could touch it. But something didn't seem right. The air was still, like some creepy horror movie. We felt sure something bad was about to happen. And it did.

We were on the highway so we couldn't turn around driving our 42-foot coach pulling a Tahoe. Paul did see two cars cross the median and turn around—but we were stuck. So we pressed on hoping the threatening weather would pass.

Suddenly, the first hail stone smashed into the windshield, cracking it. The driver's side windshield was smashed, but the passenger side windshield was okay so we could keep driving the coach. When we stopped and got out of the coach, we saw how much damage had been done to the car. The car windshield was completely smashed and the car was full of hundreds of hail stone dents. An overpass wasn't far ahead, but cars were already filling the space and the hail was already coming down hard. We had to continue driving through this icy deluge until we could find a place to pull over. For 15 minutes, it was like being shot at by a machine gun.

When the storm ended, we surveyed the damage. The hail storm destroyed all the air conditioner covers on the roof of the coach and the shower skylight as well as all the lights on the side of the coach. The ceiling vents were damaged as well. The car windshield was completely destroyed, and the body had hundreds of hail dents. I have never experienced anything like it before. We were both shaken. But we had to move forward.

We pulled into a Walmart where Paul bought a huge roll of plastic and several rolls of duct tape. He climbed on the roof and put plastic and duct tape around every opening.

I was a nervous wreck and didn't know what to do. After a while, I gathered my thoughts on a Friday afternoon about 3:00. Luckily, we had insurance, so I called our insurance agent. My advice: always carry insurance.

I realize the whole incident could have been much worse. Most important, we weren't hurt, and when we eventually returned home, the car and coach were repaired.

We continued on, all patched up, and had a great time with our family. It was definitely a trip neither of us will forget.

Chapter 8

Favorite Places

Sometimes it's fun to just keep driving and see what you find. But if you're on a limited schedule or have particular likes and dislikes, this section may help. You may prefer quiet lakes, places for children to play, historical sites, or a pleasant round of golf. Favorite Places certainly doesn't include every wonderful place in the U.S. and Canada, but it does offer a few suggestions and commentary based on my experiences and those of contributors to this book.

In some cases, names and contact information are provided. If not, refer to the Woodall's guide for the area, which you likely already own if you're a seasoned traveler.

If you have a favorite place, we'd like to hear about it and possibly share it in future editions of this book.

Northeast

NEWFOUNDLAND
N. Sydney
GULF OF
ST. LAWRENCE
Gaspé
Peninsula
Mt. Joli
Campbellton
Chatham
Prince
Edward
Island
Inverness
Cabot
Trail
Breton
Cove
Sydney
Louisbourg
Monston
Quebec
St. John
Bangor
MONTREAL
Ottawa
St. Lawrence River
Rockland
Ferry
Monhegan
Island
Portland
NOVA
SCOTIA
Halifax
Boston
Watertown
Lake
Ontario
New Bedford
Mystic
Niagara Falls
NEW YORK
Rochester
Syracuse
Buffalo
Finger Lakes

NORTHEAST

Finger Lakes Region, New York

The Finger Lakes Region offers many desirable vacation spots with pleasant summertime weather. The temperature usually hovers in the 70s at night and reaches the 80s during the day.

Phone: 1-800-548-4386. This number is the official number to get tourist and travel information about the 14 counties in the Finger Lakes.

Hejamada Campground and RV Park is about three hours from Buffalo, New York, near Cayuga Lake. This quiet campground spreads over 82 acres and offers wide sites and a variety of activities. The small lake keeps fishermen happy.

We used this campground as a base to see other Finger Lakes areas. Seneca Lake is close by, and Glenora Winery makes a good lunch stop. Many wineries dot the Finger Lakes Region.

Park website: www.hejamadacampgound.com

Phone: 315-776-5887

Wineries and winery tours: 877-424-7004.

Website: www.qualitywinetours.com for "scenic, fun, and tasteful" wine tours in the Finger Lakes Region

Niagara Falls State Park is located just off Robert Moses Parkway in the heart of downtown Niagara Falls. The American Falls, Horseshoe Falls, and Bridal Veil Falls are Must Sees. These falls are in both the U.S. and Canada.

Websites: www.niagaramovie.com or www.niagara-USA .com

Phone: 716-278-1796 for information

The Merry-Go Round Playhouse in Auburn, New York, has professional actors who travel the summer circuit. We saw *Singing in the Rain.* It was great!

Website: www.merry-go-round.com

Phone in summer: 315-255-1785

Phone in winter: 315-255-1305

Skaneateles, New York, is another Finger Lakes gem—a Must See charming town with unique shops. You might want to eat at Kabuki, a delicious sushi restaurant in Skaneateles. The phone number is 315-685-7234. The Sherwood Inn is great as well. We also enjoyed an antique boat show and a band concert by the gazebo overlooking the lake.

Sherwood Inn website: www.thesherwoodinn.com

Phone for the inn: 315-685-3405 or 1-800-374-3796

Kabuki and Sherwood Inn are under the same management.

The Corning Glass Museum in Corning, New York, presents the opportunity for a fascinating side trip. You can see "35 centuries of glass artistry, history, and technology" and watch "live, narrated glass demonstrations."

Website: www.cmog.org

Phone: 1-800-732-6845

On our way to **Sackets Harbor in upstate New York**, we stopped off at the Up The Creek Campground in Woodville, located in the Thousand Island/Seaway region of upstate New York. The hosts will make you feel right at home in their comfortable, quiet campground.

Campground website: www.upthecreekcampground.com

Phone: 315-846-5809

Just a few miles up the road from the campground is Sackets Harbor where the Battle of 1812 was fought. This historic place overlooking Lake Ontario offers year-round activities for the whole family. History buffs can visit the state battlefield site, a military cemetery, and Madison Barracks (a former military post), and enjoy live history demonstrations. Outdoor activities include picnicking, camping, golfing, sailing, power boating, kayaking, biking, and swimming at nearby beaches. Add theater and summer concerts, and you can enjoy a full agenda—or just relax and enjoy the view of Lake Ontario.

Sackets Harbor website: www.sacketsharborny.com

Sackets Harbor Visitors Center: 315-646-2321, or email shvisit@gisco.net

Massena International Kampground in upstate New York just across from Quebec, Canada, provides a first-rate experience, with spacious sites and trees everywhere.

Phone: 315-769-9483

Email: massenakamp@earthlink.net

Maine

Bar Harbor and **Acadia National Park**, located on the northeast coast of Maine, earned my four-star rating. The whole park is a treat. Bar Harbor is about 5.8 miles from Acadia National Park. It's nestled on the east side of Mount Desert Island surrounded by Acadia National Park. Cadillac Mountain on Mount Desert Island in Acadia is the highest point in Hancock County. From the top you can see Mount Katahdin, Maine's highest mountain.

Bar Harbor is a busy, commercial town full of shops and restaurants right on the coast. The fresh and tasty lobster, seafood, and chowder are outstanding. Geddy's (207-288-5077) at 19 Main St. in the heart of Bar Harbor is special. Don't miss this restaurant that serves "wood-fired" pizza, great burgers, and grilled chicken.

Many specialty shops tempt you, carrying handcrafted Maine items such as tourmaline jewelry, maple syrup, and works of local artists. One interesting shop is Window Panes (207- 288-9550), located on 166 Main Street. It features home and garden related products that are unusual and hard to find. It's called "one of Maine's coolest stores."

Bark Harbor (207-288-0404), located at 150 Main Street, sells Paw-terry clothing, towels and gifts. It also carries designer collars, leashes, toys, and all-natural treats for your favorite dog(s).

Another store you might want to check out is Jack's Jewelry (207- 288-3803), located at 23 & 27 Main Street. It's one of Maine's premier tourmaline jewelry stores. Tourmaline is Maine's state stone. Jack's has the largest collection of scarce multi-colored watermelon tourmaline.

You can choose from about a dozen campgrounds in this area (consult *Woodall's Campground Directory*). We stayed for about a week at Timberland Acres RV Park on the way to Bar Harbor and would recommend it. Hiking and biking trails abound. The weather when we were there in June was rainy and cool, but the park was still beautiful! The best time to go to Bar Harbor and Acadia is May through October.

Phone for Timberland Acres RV Park: summer, 207- 667-3600; winter, 207-667-5663

Website for Bar Harbor: www.barharborinfo.com

Website for Acadia: www.acadiainfo.com

How did Acadia become a national park? Many millionaires had homes in that area, but a fire burned them all down. The homeowners got together and decided to give the land to the National Parks. Rockefeller and others laid out the carriage roads we see today. These roads are 10 feet wide. In the winter you can cross-country ski on them, and biking is a favorite sport on the carriage roads all year long.

Camden is a quaint coastal town full of B & Bs, antiques shops, galleries, coffee houses, and restaurants serving fresh seafood. With its quintessential New England charm and numerous boats lining the harbor, it's easy to see why Camden is called The Jewel of the Maine Coast.

Website: www.camdenme.org

Rockland, another seaport town, is just a few miles south of Camden. You can catch a windjammer cruise for three to six days or for just a few hours to see the coast of Maine. Or you can sail aboard the schooner Timberwood, the only pilot schooner sailing the coast of Maine. It has no inboard engine and sails with the wind and tides in sheltered water and among the Islands of Penobscot Bay. It's an all-inclusive sailing adventure. Meals are prepared on a wood-burning cook stove. The Timberwood specializes in family cruises.

Email info@schoonertimberwind.com or call 1-800-759-9250

The joys of this culturally rich area include wonderful art museums. For example, we visited an Andrew Wyeth exhibit at one of the galleries when we were there.

Website: www.ci.rockland.me.us/

Monhegan Island is about an hour boat ride from Rockland, Maine. The cost of the ferry is nominal, and reservations aren't necessary. No cars are allowed; in fact, the island has no paved roads. About 65 people live on Monhegan Island year-round, most making their living fishing or lobstering. You can go for the day, overnight, or longer and stay in one of the hotels. The one we visited was Monhegan House, an old hotel with charming rooms that have no locks. The hotel has a big, rambling lobby with sofas for lounging in and a big, rambling porch as well.

This rugged, natural, and beautiful island has many hiking trails through wooded areas and along rocky cliffs, some of which are the highest on the Maine coastline. If you're nearby, don't miss the peacefulness of this place.

Website for Monhegan Island: www.monheganwelcome.com

Phone for Monhegan House: 207-594-7983

Vermont

Vermont's nickname is The Green Mountain State. It's a stunning state at any time, and especially in the fall when the green mountains turn to flaming red, orange, and gold with the changing of the leaves.

If you like outdoor activities such as skiing, horseback riding, and golf, Vermont is definitely worth a visit. The Green Mountains are part of the Appalachians, a mountain range that extends 250 miles from New England in the north to Georgia in the south. The Green Mountains have five peaks over 4,000 feet, and three of them sport downhill ski resorts on their slopes.

We drove up Highway 100 on the east side of the Green Mountains and down the west side. This is a good way to check out the mountains. You can make the trip in one day, but stopping off for leisurely visits takes longer so plan accordingly.

In **Manchester**, Robert Todd Lincoln, the only son of Abraham Lincoln who lived, had a summer home, Hildene. Built in 1902, this lovely mansion is chock full of historical significance for an educational experience. Manchester itself is graced with beautiful homes, shops, restaurants, B & Bs, and hotels. Don't miss it! After Manchester, you can stop in Rutland, if you're traveling north.

Website for Hildene: www.hildene.org

New Hampshire

As in all of New England, the leaves in New Hampshire are spectacular in the fall. I would recommend beginning at the White Mountains Attractions Visitor Center in North Woodstock, New Hampshire, and traveling along the White Mountains through Franconia Notch, Crawford Notch, North Conway Village, and the Kangamangus Highway. You'll be treated to seeing waterfalls, covered bridges, and scenic vistas. You can experience easy walks, strenuous hikes, golfing, live theater, and swimming at lakeside beaches.

Website: www.visitwhitemountains.com

Dixville Notch is located in the far north of New Hampshire, approximately 20 miles from Canada. We had stayed in the Timberland Camping area off Route 2 outside of Gorham (603-466-3872) and were driving through the spectacular White Mountains when suddenly a large hotel loomed out of nowhere. **The Balsams Grand Resort Hotel** signaled we were in Dixville Notch, an unincorporated village with a population of approximately 75 in the township of Coos County, New Hampshire.

Dixville Notch is known as one of the first places to declare results for the New Hampshire presidential primary and U.S. presidential elections. The tradition of the Midnight Vote was initiated in the 1960 election. How does that work? All eligible voters in the village gather at midnight in the ballroom of The Balsams Hotel to cast their ballots. One minute later, polls officially close and the results are immediately broadcast.

One of New Hampshire's surviving grand hotels, The Balsams Grand Resort Hotel is 1,800 feet above sea level and built on 15,000 acres. The resort offers golf in the summer and skiing in the winter. The two golf courses provide a view that's out of this world. In fact, from the outside balcony overlooking the golf course, you can see into Canada.

Many of the meeting rooms as well as other rooms in the hotel are elegantly furnished with lovely antiques. Oh—and our lunch was delicious.

You may not ever think of going to Dixville Notch as a destination, but if you're anywhere close, it's worth a visit. Several covered bridges nearby add to the charm of the area.

Website of The Balsams Grand Resort Hotel: www.thebalsams.com

For reservations: 877-225-7267

Another historic New Hampshire hotel is the **Mount Washington Hotel** at the Mount Washington Resort in **Bretton Woods**, which was built in 1902. Bretton Woods Ski Resort is about one and a half to two hours away from The Balsams. We didn't stay there but were very impressed by its beauty. The Mount Washington Hotel is a four-season hotel that's a favorite retreat of presidents, poets, and celebrities. The hotel has enchanting music, excellent dining, and luxurious décor. It offers many amenities, such as indoor and outdoor pools, Jacuzzis, and fireplaces. The hotel's elegant dining room serves four-course dinners with orchestra accompaniment nightly.

Website: www.mountwashingtonresort.com

Phone: 603-278-1000

In **North Conway**, we saw the Neil Simon play Chapter Two and greatly enjoyed it. We love the theater. Every time we get a chance, we go. As you travel, check out the events of the town you're in. The theater in small towns is usually quite good. Attending a play will provide a break in the routine, which we find makes the adventure even more fun.

The historic and charming town of **Littleton** near Twin Mountain was noted by *Outside Magazine* in 1905 as one of the most interesting small towns. We agreed. One feature we liked was the Healthy Rhino health food store in Littleton. Located on the banks of the Ammonoosuc River is the Littleton Grist Mill. This historic mill first opened in 1798 and has been fully restored to its original appearance. Between 1867 and 1909, the local Kilburn Brothers factory published photographs called stereoviews and sold stereoscopes, which were picture viewers popular in the Victorian Age that created a 3D effect.

Massachusetts

Boston is a city where you don't want to drive if you can possibly avoid it. Traffic is ferocious; streets are crowded with people as well. We took the commuter train from Braintree just outside Boston to Park Street where the Freedom Trail begins.

The Freedom Trail is a 2.5 mile red-brick walking trail (also called the Red Line) that takes you through various parts of the downtown area and the historic district to 16 nationally significant historic sites. On the Red Line, you'll see The Old North Church where Paul Revere held up the lantern to signal that the British were coming. The USS Constitution is also on the Red Line and can be visited by tourists. The JFK Library is quite impressive with its unusual architecture. It's built on the water where JFK's sailboat is displayed. The memorabilia about his life and presidential years as well as movie clips of his and Jackie's life are a touching slice of history. This impressive library is a Must See if you're anywhere near Boston.

Plymouth is a quaint town on the Atlantic Ocean between Boston and Cape Cod, Martha's Vineyard, and Nantucket. **Plymouth Rock** is where the Mayflower landed. Pinewood Campground, just outside of Plymouth, has big pine trees and spacious campsites. Highly recommended, it's located on the shore of Plymouth Harbor, on the ocean and near a beach.

We took the Ferry from Plymouth to the island of **Martha's Vineyard** and spent the day there. I recommend the Island Tour as a good overview. I was impressed by the island's beauty and the surrounding ocean. Water has always appealed to me. I find it very peaceful. Martha's Vineyard has beautiful beaches, and I loved the gingerbread cottages, too.

Note: We find that staying in one place for four to five days allows us to get to know the area. Longer visits can be extremely educational as well as relaxing. The Boston area and Plymouth, as well as the area around Bar Harbor, Maine, were three of the places we hung out for a while.

New Bedford is 50 miles south of Boston. **The Whaling Museum** in New Bedford has just been remodeled and boasts the largest Blue Whale Skeleton in the world. The textile mills were also located in New Bedford. People from Ireland and England came over to New Bedford, and the cotton mills supported the immigrants with jobs. The Wamsutta Mills, which made men's shirts and sheets, moved south in the early 1950s because it was cheaper to produce these items in the South. New Bedford is a beautiful sea coast town definitely worth a visit.

Fairhaven had a benefactor, Henry Huttleston Rogers, who built the library, town hall, and all the elementary schools. The high school, known as the Castle on the Hill, had its own china and stained glass Tiffany windows. Historic Fort Phoenix, built to protect the settlers from the British, still stands, cannon and all. The Fort is on a state beach where people can swim and clam bakes are popular.

Rhode Island

The Mansions of Newport were built by the Vanderbilts and coal and railroad tycoons in the 19th century (before taxes!). These mansions and furnishings come straight out of storybook lifestyles of yesteryear. Newport is a town cut out for walking, with many great restaurants and unique shops. Be sure to tour at least one or two of these mansions. One in particular sticks out in my mind. The Breakers was the historic Vanderbilt summer "cottage." It's now visited by more than a third of a million people every year. Built in Italian Renaissance style, The Breakers is viewed by scholars as a cultural icon of its time. It boasts 70 rooms, which held furnishings and fixtures with a Parisian influence. In 1972, the Preservation Society purchased the house from heirs, and in 1984, The Breakers was opened to visitors to raise money for its upkeep. Today the mansion is designated a National Historic Landmark.

Connecticut

Historic **Mystic Seaport** is right on the water and "overflowing" with boats—from the 1800s fishing boats in the renowned marine museum to tall ships and other sailing vessels and current pleasure boats in the harbor. Mystic has its own shipyard to restore and repair ships. If you tire of marveling at the marine exhibits, you can meander through a 19th century seafaring village and see what homes and shops looked like back then. If you enjoy history, boats, and great little shops, or just want to try out the Mystic Pizza made famous by the movie of the same name, visit Mystic Seaport.

Websites: www.mystic.org or www.mysticseaport.org

The **Pequot Museum** is only 20 minutes from Mystic. The largest Native American Museum in America, it's a Must See for a total-immersion education, the view from the high tower, and its delightful gift shop. If you have children along, they'll love it. The museum includes a life-size village and many interactive, kid-friendly areas.

Website: www.pequotmuseum.org

Located on the same property but down the road is the famed **Foxwoods Casino** run by the same tribe that owns the museum, the Mashantucket Pequot Tribal Nation. Whether you're a gambler or just want to check out this giant complex of six casinos and the world's largest bingo hall, it will likely blow you away.

Website: www.foxwoods.com

Groton, a short drive from the other Connecticut sights mentioned, is home to the **Nautilus**, the first nuclear-powered submarine, which was retired in 1980 and designated a National Historic Landmark in 1982. You can visit the Submarine Force Library and Museum to learn more than you ever wanted to know about submarines. We enjoyed seeing the Nautilus but didn't tour the library and museum.

Website: www.ussnautilus.org

EAST

Gettysburg, Pennsylvania

Gettysburg is a monumental site in American history. The Civil War, fought in 1863, comes alive when you visit Gettysburg. Lincoln's "Four Score and Seven Years Ago" speech becomes real when you stand on the exact spot where he gave this memorable address. An electric map points out the strategies between the Confederate Army of the South and the Union Army of the North, and a driving tour of the entire battle is available.

The cemetery is beautifully laid out, and magnificent bronze statues of the many majors and generals involved in the war accentuate the cemetery grounds and the many battlefields. We saw a diorama of Pickett's Charge. This battle literally decided the outcome of the war and resulted in the death of all 5,000 of his men within 15 minutes.

You likely studied this in history class, but being there and seeing the place with your own eyes gives a deeper meaning to the facts and figures. It's difficult to believe that the Battle of Gettysburg was decided in only three days, July 1-3, 1863.

The museum at the visitor's center houses memorabilia collected by the families of Civil War Veterans. The entire town of Gettysburg is a walk into the past. The houses are built very close together and have a style of their own. All in all, we found two days in Gettysburg highly worthwhile.

Website: www.gettysburgfoundation.org

SOUTH AND SOUTHEAST

Florida

Sarasota is our favorite place in Florida. We recommend Sun-N-Fun, Florida's friendliest RV resort, which has more than 1,800 RV sites, each with full hookup, cable TV, and a picnic table. Park models (as well as small vacation homes) are available to purchase or rent.

Sun-N-Fun has many activities, including dances once a month and other entertainment at reasonable prices. The resort offers an Olympic-size swimming pool, tennis courts, lawn bowling, and bocce ball as well.

Sun-N-Fun website: www.sunnfunfl.com

Phone: 1-800-843-2421

The city of Sarasota provides the ultimate in cultural activities: plays, live theater, a famous circus. About a century ago, in 1910, brothers John and Charles Ringling decided to invest in the future of Sarasota. These two of the five original Ringling brothers turned a small traveling circus into an international entertainment empire. They had incredible influence on the economy, development, and culture of the quaint village on beautiful Sarasota Bay. John and Charles bought 67,000 acres, which are now Sarasota and Longboat Key, as investment property.

When the Ringling Bros. and Barnum and Bailey Circus moved into its winter quarters in 1927, it attracted circus families and artists from around the world. Sarasota became known as Circus City USA. The John and Mable Ringling Museum of Art as well as opera are available to enjoy throughout the winter season.

The weather in Sarasota is ideal for lounging on nearby beaches. St. Armand's Circle offers stores and restaurants for every taste and pocketbook. You won't be sorry if you stop by Sarasota for a month—or for the whole winter!

Our Favorite Campgrounds and Places to Go

Here's a list of favorite places to camp and stay in Texas, Louisiana, North Carolina, Florida, and—well, okay, it's not South or Southeast, but—Ohio from a couple who sent it to us.

1. Number one on our list has to be **Bayview RV Resort in Rockport, Texas**. Rockport is close to Corpus Christi. The restaurants and shopping are the finest around, and if fishing or golf is your pleasure, you certainly won't be bored. The campground features two clubhouses, two pools, putt-putt golf, and many other activities to keep you busy.

2. Number two on our list is the **Rio Grande Valley of Texas**—with restaurants, flea markets, shopping, and more. If that's not enough, you can take an all-day sightseeing trip to Mexico. If you're near McAllen or Brownsville, Texas, pop over the border to Monterrey. If you're near El Paso, cross over to Juarez, Mexico.

3. Number three is **Abita Springs, Louisiana**, which is just north of New Orleans. It's an older town to see and explore. Many outdoor opportunities are offered by Fairview-Riverside State Park. You can enjoy beaches, breweries, and restaurants. Lake Pontchartrain connects Abita Springs and New Orleans. Lake Pontchartrain is 41 miles long and 25 miles wide. The Pontchartrain Causeway was opened in 1969 and takes about a half hour to cross, so you can visit New Orleans for the day. New Orleans is known as a "joy of life" attraction. You can start with The French Quarter, which offers renowned jazz and sumptuous dining.

4. Number four is **Helen, Georgia**, a touristy type of town with quaint little shops similar to Alpine villages in Switzerland tucked into the Blue Ridge Mountains along the Chattahoochee River. From cobblestone streets to Old World architecture, the town faithfully portrays traditional Bavarian style. It also hosts a six-week Octoberfest, which offers Bavarian beer, schnitzel, dancing, and lots of polka music. The large windmill on the edge of town and the waterfalls around the area make it a camera buff's dream.

5. Number five on our list is **Franklin, North Carolina.** The cool mountain air, sightseeing, and gem mining make visiting there different and pleasant. Franklin is the gem capital of the world, with a

Gem and Mineral Museum and an abundance of gem shops. The town also offers a unique fire tower that provides breathtaking views of three counties and a Family Entertainment Center with bowling, a pool parlor, and pinball machines. Don't miss Cullasaja Falls and the gem mines including Cowee Mountain Ruby Mine, Rocky Face Gem Mine, Rose Creek Mine, and Mason's Ruby and Sapphire Mine. The area also provides plenty of opportunities for outdoor recreation.

6. Cross over the Smoky Mountains from North Carolina and you come to number six on our list, **Gatlinburg, Tennessee**. You can explore a Civil War battlefield, mosey around flea markets, and much more. Civil War battlefields can be found all across Tennessee as well as in Virginia, Georgia, Pennsylvania, Ohio, Missouri, Mississippi, Alabama, and Arkansas. Just five minutes from Gatlinburg is Pigeon Forge with its outlet malls, old country-style restaurants, and (we can't forget!) Dollywood, a theme park owned by Dolly Parton. Dollywood is the great Smoky Mountains family fun vacation adventure with shows, festivals, roller coasters, kiddie rides, themed shops, dining, and more.

7. The seventh place on our list has to be **Florida**, with all its beautiful beaches. We especially like the **Titusville area** and the **Space Coast National Parks**, including 13 beaches where you can swim

or surf fish. We like to try our luck fishing, talk with people we meet, have a light lunch, then walk in the surf. The spaceport Cape Canaveral is close by and has enough displays to keep a person busy all day.

8. **Lake Okeechobee in South Florida** makes the list as number eight. You can walk or shop, whatever your pleasure. Going to flea markets on the weekends is a fun pastime and a way to meet people and view their wares. We've always found something we couldn't live without—new or used. You could take months exploring all the small towns around the lake.

9. **Saint Augustine, Florida**, is number nine. The beaches are fabulous for swimming or sunbathing. Or you can cross over the Bridge of Lions into the old city where the quaint shops seem to transport you back in time. Don't forget the fort, built in 1756. Fort Marion was built of coquina (a shell of natural formation found only on the eastern coast of Florida). Walking through the cemetery reading the headstones in such an old city may give you an eerie feeling, as it did us. Sample the local fare and gather memories for a lifetime.

MIDWEST

Missouri

Meramec State Park in Missouri spreads over 6,896 acres. It offers camping and scenic float trips down the meandering Meramec River. You can explore four well-known caves, go fishing or hiking, and eat at the park restaurant if you don't feel like cooking. This park is a favorite in Missouri for canoeists and fishermen.

Directions: From St. Louis, take Hwy 44 west to Sullivan, Missouri. At exit 226, follow Hwy 185 south for five miles to the park entrance on the right. Stop at the visitor center for maps and trail information.

Phone: 573-468-6072

The Ozark National Scenic Riverways area has two of the finest canoeing rivers in the Midwest. The spring-fed Current and Jacks Fork rivers with their accompanying parks and campgrounds provide fun ways to get closer to nature and bring families together. The Ozark National Scenic Riverways is located in the southern part of Missouri off Highway 60, Van Buren, Missouri.

- **Round Springs** campground along the Current River is a popular camping destination in the Ozark National Scenic Riverways. Water is turned off from October 30 to April 15.

  Website: www.missouriscenicrivers.com

  Phone: 877-444-6777

- **Alley Springs** is open all year. Water is turned off from October 30 to April 15.

  Phone: 573-323-4236

- **Big Spring** is the largest single-orifice freshwater spring in the U.S. and one of the largest in the world. Nearby is Big Spring State Park, which offers picnicking, hiking areas, and a campground. Water is turned off from October 15 to April 15.

  Directions: From St. Louis, the area is best reached via I44. Take State Route 68 south from St. James. Then take State Route 19 south into the park.

  Website: www.stateparks.com/usa.html for information about U.S. state parks.

  Phone for Big Spring Campground information: 573-323-4236 between 8 a.m. and 4:30 p.m. CST week days

Note: The main roads throughout the park are well maintained state highways, but they're hilly and winding, so be careful and take your time. Roads to the back country areas are typically dirt and not as well maintained. Some are suitable for passenger cars and RVs, some are not. Ask at the ranger stations for driving conditions. Dirt roads may get muddy, or even washed out at times by storms.

St. Louis, The Gateway to the West, offers history, interesting architecture, cultural events, and great sports. I recommend RVers stay at the **Casino Queen RV Park** or Hotel in East St. Louis, in Illinois, just across the Mississippi River from downtown St. Louis. The park has large sites and can accommodate all sizes of RVs. Most of the places listed below are in the downtown or midtown area of the city.

Address of Casino Queen RV Park: 200 S. Front Street, East St. Louis, IL 62201

Phone: 314-241-2628 or toll free 1-800-777-0777

If you're staying in St. Louis a while, don't miss these highlights:

- **Must see! The Jefferson National Expansion Memorial**, where you'll see the **Gateway Arch** designed by Eero Saarinen that's 630 feet tall. You can ride to the top of the arch and see for miles in both Missouri and Illinois. The underground museum features a trip through history and is a treat for both adults and children.

- Near the Arch is the **Old Court House**, where the historic Dred Scott case of 1847 was tried. The Old Court House is now part of the Jefferson Memorial Expansion (314-655-1700). It offers an 18-minute film of the Dred Scott case.

- Also nearby is the **Old Cathedral Basilica** of St. Louis, King of France. The Old Cathedral (209 Walnut Street; 314-231-3250) is now known as the Basilica of St. Louis, King. The city of St. Louis was founded by the French, who came up from New Orleans and founded St. Louis in 1764. It was named after King Louis IX, the most famous king of France. He was a friend to the poor his entire life, dying at the age of 41.

What I like about the Old Cathedral is its setting on the Mississippi River as well as its simplicity. I also like the fact that those who run the Cathedral continue to help the poor and homeless in the neighborhood on a regular basis. The New Cathedral, located at 4445 Lindell Boulevard in St. Louis, has more mosaics than any Cathedral in the world. A visit to the special New Cathedral is one to be remembered.

- If you are a major league baseball fan, check out the **Cardinals**. For tickets to games: www.stlcardinals.com/tickets

  All of the above are within easy walking distance of each other and near the Mississippi River.

- A few blocks away from the river is the restored **Union Station** where all the trains came into St. Louis. Now the Station includes a hotel, restaurants, and shops. Be sure to see the lobby. Built in 1894, Union Station was redone on 1985 and has become the largest "reuse" project in the United States. It was designed by Theodore C. Link at the cost of 6.5 million dollars. The Station has a 65-foot tall barrel-vaulted ceiling. Link got his ideas from the south of France and the building reflects Victorian design.

- The **Fox Theater** on Grand Avenue has been completely restored (over-the-top decorated). It's home to Broadway productions as well as specialty performances from well-known artists and features one of the few remaining giant Wurlitzer theatre organs from the days of silent films. Tours are available.

- For a musical evening, the **St. Louis Symphony Orchestra** is world class and just down the street from the Fox Theater. Local jazz clubs are in the same neighborhood.

- **Forest Park** is one of the largest urban parks in the U.S. With 1,293 acres of land and numerous attractions, the park is one of St. Louis's most treasured resources. It's not "just" a park! Forest Park offers:

  - The **Science Center**. Located at 5050 Oakland; www.slsc.org; phone 314-289-4400.

  - The **Muny Opera**. Offering outdoor musicals from June through August.

  - The **St. Louis Zoo**. One of the best in the world, this zoo houses 5,000 animals on 90 acres, with a children's zoo and a miniature train to ride to each area. Located at 1 Government Drive; www.stlzoo.org; phone 314-781-0900.

  - The **St. Louis Art Museum**. This museum contains more than 100 galleries. The main building was part of the 1904 World's Fair.

Located in Forest Park by the zoo. Phone 314-721-0072.

- The **Missouri History Society** with the **Jefferson Memorial Building**, including a marble statue of our country's third president. Located at 5700 Lindell Boulevard; www.mohistory.org; phone 314-746-4599.
- The **Jewel Box.** This marvel of glass architecture is filled with flowers year-round. On the National Historic Register and recently renovated, the Jewel Box was built by the city in 1936 and sits on a 17-acre site in Forest Park.
- If you play golf, you can choose from **several golf courses** in Forest Park.

- Farther away from the river is the **Missouri Botanical Garden**, one of the top three botanical gardens in the world and another Must See in St. Louis. You'll find something for everyone in the family. If you have difficulty walking, they have a lovely tram tour with a guide. Just sit and enjoy. Website: www.mobot.org

Especially for children but fun for adults, too:

- The **City Museum** is an amazing museum for the young and the young at heart. There's fun for everyone. Lots of climbing and crawling opportunities and slides made of a variety of materials. One is made from conveyer rollers. The architecture of the City Museum is breathtaking. Located at 701 N. 15th Street; www.citymuseum.org.

- The **Magic House** is a hands-on learning experience for children. It provides a safe, stimulating environment where families can learn together. Located at 516 S. Kirkwood Road; www.magichouse.org; phone 314-822-8900.
- **Six Flags** is a theme park that has great shows and awesome rides. Check the website or call for season opening and closing times. Website: www.sixflags.com; phone 636-938-4800.
- **Grant's Farm** was the farm of former president Ulysses S. Grant. It's fun for the whole family, featuring a variety of animals on display. Small children can see the animals through the fences. Located at 10501 Gravois Road; www.grantsfarm.com; phone 314-843-1700.

Illinois

Springfield is a one-and-a-half-hour drive from St. Louis along Highway 55. The **Abraham Lincoln Presidential Library** is a Must See. It's the world's largest collection of documentary material related to the life of Abraham Lincoln, our country's 16th president. The Library includes an activity area for children that's a unique experience. The Presidential Museum and Library has a hub-and-spoke arrangement. That means all galleries are arranged around a central hub, or orientation point (the plaza). You'll see: 1) a crude cabin representing Lincoln's early years, 2) a display of his presidential years, 3) the Union Theater, and 4) a display regarding Lincoln's family. All in all, the Lincoln Presidential Museum and Library has been well planned. It's a special place to remember a great president and his importance in the history of the United States. Be sure to see both of the 15-minute shows—they'll blow you away! And you can take a photo of your family with "the Lincolns."

Located at 112 N. Sixth Street downtown. The hours are 9 a.m. to 5 p.m. daily.

Phone: 217-558-8844

Kansas

Abilene, Kansas, is great for a one- or two-day visit. As the former home of former president Dwight D. Eisenhower, it offers many historical sites and a presidential museum. A brightly painted trolley circles the town and picks up people staying at B & Bs and campgrounds. It's great to hop on and take a tour without having to drive! In addition to a number of museums, Abilene is dotted with attractive old homes with wide, inviting porches.

Ohio

Conneaut, Ohio. We were on our way to Buffalo for an RV rally, and we were lucky to find the lovely **Evergreen Lake Park** campground in Conneaut, just outside **Cleveland**. Trees are abundant, and the weather was comfortably cool when we were there in August. Nearby Lake Erie offers the opportunity to walk on the beach, fly a kite, or just enjoy the water. We did it all.

Located off Highway 90, 80 miles from Cleveland and 35 miles from Erie, Pennsylvania. Phone: 440-599-8802

Wisconsin

Door County, Wisconsin, is a popular Great Lakes vacation and tourist area; it's definitely one of our favorites. A 75-mile-long peninsula bordered by the waters of Green Bay on the west and Lake Michigan on the east, it's spectacular in every season. The more than 300 miles of picturesque shoreline ensure you're always near a relaxing water view. Ten lighthouses guard the harbors and the 40-plus islands of the county. In fact, Door County boasts more lighthouses, miles of shoreline, and state parks than any other county in the United States.

Small towns, shops, and art galleries line the peninsula. In the spring, when the apple and cherry trees burst into gorgeous bloom, you can enjoy the Festival of Blossoms. Spring also brings a special lighthouse showcase. In the summer, every community comes alive with activities, including water sports of every kind, concerts, music, and fish boils. Renowned painters, potters, and performing art troupes are at your disposal.

Door County offers hiking, biking, a challenging golf course, world class symphony music, antique stores, nature preserves, and great restaurants for every taste. It's easy to see why *Money Magazine* named Door County "one of the top 10 vacation destinations in North America."

Website: www.doorcounty.com/

Egg Harbor in Door County was named for a legendary 1825 egg-throwing battle between two boat crews headed into the harbor. This picturesque village is home to the Birch Creek Music Center where you can enjoy evening concerts in the "barn." In the downtown district, you can find shops, galleries, and restaurants to delight your palate and your pocketbook. A favorite event in the fall is the annual Pumpkin Patch Festival, held on Columbus Day weekend in October.

We had never been to the Upper Peninsula, but we'd heard about the museum at **Whitefish Point**—truly one of our most memorable places. It's called the Great Lakes Shipwreck Museum, a maritime museum in the Upper Peninsula.

Whitefish Point forms the entrance to Lake Superior's Whitefish Bay. The site of the oldest active lighthouse on Lake Superior, it was first lit in 1849. Whitefish Point shares honors with the lighthouse at Copper Harbor for having the first lights on Lake Superior.

Whitefish Point is also known as the graveyard of ships because more vessels have been lost here than in any other part of the lake. Hundreds of vessels including the famed Edmond Fitzgerald lie on the bottom of the bay. Appropriately, as you enter the museum, you hear Gordon Lightfoot singing "The Wreck of the Edmond Fitzgerald" and it plays while you tour the museum. The museum is very interesting and educational.

After thoroughly enjoying Whitefish Point and the museum, we walked on the beach and saw posters of all the men who had gone down with the Edmond Fitzgerald. Very moving.

Whitefish Point is approximately 70 miles from Sault St. Marie. Take Hwy M-123 to Paradise, then north on Whitefish Point Road for 11 miles. For more information, contact Great Lakes Shipwreck Historical Society at 906-635-1742 or 800-635-1742, or call the Shipwreck Museum at 906-492-3747 during the summer.

When we stopped at a small restaurant in the area, a gentleman there recommended going to Copper Harbor in the Upper Peninsula. He said the best restaurant ever was up there right on Lake Superior.

Copper Harbor in Michigan's Upper Peninsula is one of our all-time favorites. The views of magnificent Lake Superior will remain in our memories forever.

Chances are you'll find something that suits your fancy in Copper Harbor. You can charter a boat or go hiking, kayaking, canoeing, fishing, agate hunting, or berry picking. The Keweenaw Mountain Lodge features a beautiful and challenging golf course. Or you can even explore the woods and the numerous beaches in and around the town.

A gentleman we met in Whitefish Point recommended the Harbor Haus with its expansive view of Copper Harbor, reportedly the best restaurant in the Upper Peninsula. He was right on. We dined there three nights in a row. The cuisine is German—hence the name. The restaurant is famous for its cheese soup and tasty fresh lake trout caught that day, which we recommend. We also recommend the chocolate torte.

If you dine there, see if you can time your visit to witness this tradition: Whenever the Isle Royale Queen returns to the harbor, Harbor Haus waitresses rush outside and perform a Rockette-like routine.

Harbor Haus: 77 Brockway Avenue, Copper Harbor, MI
Phone: 906-289-4502

We found Copper Harbor to be an exceptionally worthwhile and memorable place to visit. The best time to go is mid-May to mid-October. Whatever time of year, bring layers of clothing so you're prepared for changing weather.

As we traveled north in Michigan, we had the opportunity to take our bikes on the ferry out to **Mackinac Island**, where motor vehicles have been banned for more than a century. We greatly enjoyed biking around the downtown district and the Mackinac State Historic Park.

The island offers a spectrum of sights, from blacksmith demonstrations at the Benjamin Blacksmith Shop to tropical gardens and hundreds of butterflies at the Butterfly House and the Wings of Mackinac Butterfly Conservatory. The butterfly exhibits are open May through October. For a totally different experience, you can visit Fort Mackinac, open June through August.

Paul and I decided to go our separate ways and meet at a designated place after a few hours. We both got lost—well, maybe I was the one who got lost. At any rate, we had a miscommunication. What should I do? Paul was wearing a Spiderman bike shirt that day, so I parked myself at a crossroads and kept asking people if they'd seen a guy in a Spiderman bike shirt. As it got later and later, I became worried because it was about time to catch the ferry. I rode into town to wait at the pier—and there, at last, was Paul. All's well that ends well.

Website: www.mackinacisland.org/

SOUTHWEST

Northern Utah

Salt Lake City is historically interesting and beautiful. If you're a skier, you'll love skiing the mountains. Mormon history abounds in this city. If you go, don't miss seeing Temple Square and hearing the world famous **Mormon Tabernacle Choir**, known as "America's Choir." The Choir gives weekly concerts and rehearsals that are open to the public.

The Mormon Tabernacle Choir is located at 50 West South Temple.

Choir website: www.mormontabernaclechoir.org

Salt Lake City: www.slcgov.com/visitors

Park City is a charming town and a great base for skiing. The main street is reminiscent of a small Western town you'd see in the movies. The Sundance Film Festival started by Robert Redford in 1985 is held here. Movie stars arrive in Park City during January when the festival takes place. A different movie is played every night for a month. Check the Sundance Institute website for specific dates.

Website: www.sundance.org

The **Eccles Theater** is a privately funded Performing Arts Foundation dedicated to bringing world class performances to Park City. If you're in the area and are interested in the theater, call ahead to find out what performances will be available.

The theater is located at 1750 Kearns Boulevard.

Website: www.ecclescenter.org

Phone: 435-655-3114

Park City also has a variety of B & Bs, condos, and other accommodations for skiers and other visitors to the area. It's a fun town whether you ski or not.

Other Parts of Utah

In my opinion, Utah is one of the most beautiful places I've ever experienced. It's America's national parks capital with five national parks, including:

- Zion National Park
- Bryce Canyon National Park
- Arches National Park
- Canyonlands National Park
- Capital Reef National Park

(For Utah travel information: 1-800-200-1160.)

Moab in southeastern Utah along the Colorado River is a resort town with beautiful natural surroundings. It has an arts community, a music festival in September, and a folk festival in November.

In Moab, you can indulge in activities such as biking, hiking, four-wheeling, river rafting, golfing, and horseback riding—or you can take a ride in a Hummer or a jet boat.

If you go there, be sure to stop at the Moab Information Center for information on activities and accommodations.

*Note: Also be sure to consult **Woodall's Campground Directory**. You can purchase a directory for North America or a specific region at Camping World all over the U.S.*

Website: www.woodalls.com

Phone: 805-667-4100

Arches National Park is only five miles north of Moab. This scenic park is chock full of sandstone formations, making it a unique adventure for visitors. You can easily see the park by car, bike, or hiking trails. Slick Rock bike trail is 10.3 miles long—a half-day loop that's a mountain biking mecca. The southwestern United States presents a world of stone and sky. Over time, nature has created a wondrous landscape inhabited by many animals who have adapted to the dry climate and wildly varying temperatures. You'll be amazed at the panorama of buttes, canyons, plateaus, and of course, natural arches. Rock climbers ply their skill scaling the formations. Hiking trails lead to enormous rocks balanced on thin spires. The artistic nature of the rocks and the cliff walls that tower hundreds of feet into the blue sky present a paradise for photographers. Arches National Park ranks as a top favorite place to visit in Utah.

Website: www.nps.gov/arch/

Phone for visitor information: 435-719-2299

Canyonlands National Park, the largest national park in state of Utah, is 35 miles west of Moab.

We have a dear friend, Charlie Cramer, who's one of the best photographers in the world. He gave us a list of special places to see and experience as we traveled in the Utah area. He suggested we not miss the Shafer Trail in Canyonlands National Park.

One morning, we packed our lunch and headed for Canyonlands. We paid our four dollars to get into the park, and 50 feet beyond the visitor's booth a sign read "The Shafer

Trail." Because Charlie had suggested this, I told Paul we should see it and "get it over with."

What a treat! We saw some of the most exciting canyons and rock formations we'd ever experienced. "Big Red" (as we had named our maroon Tahoe) got a workout that day. We ended up driving in four-wheel drive over the extremely treacherous terrain. The car leaned at 90-degree angles all the way down the canyon. It was terribly exciting but also terribly scary for me. Of course, Paul loved every minute of it.

A side note I will never forget: I had to go the bathroom really badly. We'd finally reached the bottom of the Shafer Trail. I waited and waited to find a "Johnny on the Spot." Not a sign of a potty. Paul said, "Go on and go; no one's anywhere around for miles." Or so he thought. Not two minutes after I finished, up drove three vehicles. Oh well. Then—wouldn't you know—just a little way down the road, we came upon a bathroom.

We continued on the road, which took us through the town of Potash. The term "potash" comes from the pioneer practice of extracting potassium fertilizer by leaching wood ashes and evaporating the solution in large iron pots. The paved road ends at the Moab Salt Plant where potash is extracted. Potash is also the common name given to potassium carbonate and various mined and manufactured salts that contain the element potassium. It's been used in the manufacture of glass, soap, and soil fertilizer. Potash-bearing rock deposits occur in many regions of the world.

On the Moab Scenic Auto Tours, you can enjoy a spectacular drive on the La Sal Mountain Loop. Also in this area are petroglyphs carved in the rock by the Indians about

1,000 years ago. Petroglyphs are ancient symbols that tell a story. You can get information about both the petroglyphs and potash from the visitor center booth.

It took us a few hours for this educational drive through the canyon. We didn't have to drive out the way we came in. All in all, it turned out to be a spectacular and exciting four-wheeling day.

Website: www.nps.gov/cany/

Phone for visitor information: 435-719-2313

Dead Horse Point State Park is nine miles north Moab on SR 313, 18 miles off Hwy 191. It's one of Utah's most spectacular state parks, towering on a rock promontory 2,000 feet above the Colorado River. It provides a breathtaking panorama of canyons, sculpted pinnacles, and buttes. The park is named Dead Horse because cowboys used to corral wild mustangs on the Point, leaving the unwanted ones to find their way back to the open mesas. Legend has it, a band of them didn't leave and died there of thirst. The visitor's center, interpretive museum, developed campground, and overlook shelter make this park comfortable and informative as well as spectacular.

Website: www.utah.com/stateparks/dead_horse.htm

Moab Area Travel Council: 1-800-635-6622

Capitol Reef National Park, located in south central Utah about 60 miles south of I-70, is another place you don't want to miss. We got a driving map from the visitor center, which also explained how the rock was formed. "Reef" describes a 100-mile long ridge of rock that was thrust up from the earth millions of years ago. "Capitol" derives from a rock formation resembling the U.S. Capitol building in Washington, D.C. The rock formations here were also sandstone. Erosion has created marvelously colored and wildly varied rock formations of great beauty out of the ridge. Capitol Reef is isolated, which makes it the least visited of Utah's national parks.

Website: www.nps.gov/care/

Six miles from Capitol Reef, we found a trailer park in Torrey called **Thousand Lakes RV Park.** It's located one mile west of Torrey on Hwy 24.

Phone for reservations: 1-800-355-8995.

Calf Creek Falls is located 15 miles east of the town of Escalante on Highway 12. Elevation there is 5,346 feet. The **Calf Creek Campground** is between Boulder, Utah, and Escalante, an area also recommended by Charlie Cramer. The hike to Calf Creek Falls is reportedly only two and a half miles each way. We didn't believe that after hiking for four and a half hours round trip. It was worth it, though, to enjoy the spectacular scenery around every turn.

We camped at a campground right on Calf Creek. In fact, our bedroom overlooked Calf Creek. It was very challenging to get to the site because Paul had to maneuver our coach across a creek flowing with two feet of water. But he did it, and luckily he didn't scrape the bottom of the coach. The campground was perfect, though. Full hookups and conveniently located. We've been extremely lucky to find perfect campgrounds.

Again following Charlie's suggestion, we hiked the Queen Garden Trail, which started and ended at Sunrise Point. It was one and a half miles long. Going down it was easy, but we did lots of puffing coming back up. We made it and felt proud of ourselves.

Another 18 miles down the canyon, we stopped at Inspiration Point, which was also one of our favorites. It can actually be reached by a day trip from Salt Lake City. People climb 4,000 feet traveling the Willard Scenic Backway, which ends at Inspiration Point on 9,422-foot Willard Mountain. With its combination of geological formations, colors, and light and shadows, Inspiration Point is one of the most amazing sights we've ever seen.

Bryce Canyon National Park is yet another stunning sight. Erosion has shaped colorful limestone, sandstone, and mudstone into thousands of spires, pinnacles, and mazes called "hoodoos." The walls are red and the peaks are white, which gives the scene a "castle-like" look.

Website: www.nps.gov/brca/

Zion National Park has the "wow" effect. We could hardly believe our eyes. It was so beautiful, we had to blink to make sure we weren't dreaming. We stopped at Cinemax at the visitor's center to get the history and background of Zion National Park, and I would recommend taking in this experience.

Again, Charlie was right. The **Zion Narrows** is one of the best, if not the best, hike in the National Park System. The **Temple of Sinawava Trail** is about one mile long and fabulous. The trail begins outside the east entrance of the park on the top of the mesa. Ride from the entrance of Zion on the paved Pa'ius Trail for 1.8 miles, then take the shuttle from the Canyon Junction stop to the last stop at Temple of Sinawava Trail. If you like hiking and caves, you can take advantage of more than 18 miles of hiking trails into lava caves.

We crossed the Virgin River at a place where aboriginal Indians held their special ceremonies. That wasn't in our plan, and our shoes got wet because we didn't take them off. Then the trail took us alongside the river. The Narrows Trail continued for another 16 miles, but we just walked until we arrived at the **Emerald Pool**, about a one-mile hike. Overall, we hiked for about two miles, and every view was a sight to behold.

Paul and I agree that Zion is one of our favorite places ever. Thank you, Dear God, for such a place and for the opportunity to see Your Hands at work. Wow! Life is great!

We then headed for Lake Powell, stopping along the way at **Buckskin Gulch**, another Charlie Cramer suggestion. We approached the ranger station for a map and directions. The ranger scared us a little by saying, "Go at your own risk. Turn back if it starts raining."

We started our hike and saw some of the most fabulous slot canyons imaginable. The slot canyons were formed when rivers cut through the soft limestone, twisting and turning, and creating high, sheer walls alive with incredible colors and formations. Then it started raining, and I wanted to go back. But, did we? No. Not Paul. He said, "It's just a few drops." Luckily, nothing happened and we eventually made it back safely.

On this trip, I started to like four-wheeling. We took a nine-mile ride up and down the gulch, but we had to walk at least two to three miles each way into and out of the deepest part of the gulch. When we arrived back at the top of the nine-mile dirt road, we picked up Merrily (our coach) and drove on toward Lake Powell.

That night we stayed at the **Wahweap RV Park** in Lake Powell. The park overlooks the harbor at Lake Powell with all the fancy houseboats. House boating is big at Lake Powell.

Phone for reservations: 888-896-3829

Antelope Canyon is on the Navaho Reservation. Charlie has many beautiful photographs of Antelope Canyon, but the real thing is indescribable. The Navajo Indians charged us fifteen dollars each to bus over to the canyon where people can stay for a maximum of two hours. We didn't stay that long, but Paul bought me a beautiful bear necklace and earrings made out of many different kind of stones—malachite, turquoise, lapis, and a few others. The necklace looks like a colorful puzzle. Bears symbolize strength and are sacred to the Indians. I'm so lucky to be spoiled rotten!

At **Antelope Canyon, Antelope Canyon Narrows** on the Navaho Reservation near Page, Arizona, is a spiritual place for the Indians. Buses pick visitors up from the parking lot and take them to and from the Narrows. Antelope Canyon is the most visited and most photographed slot canyon in the American Southwest. It includes two separate visual experiences, referred to respectively as Upper Antelope Canyon, or The Crack, and Lower Antelope Canyon, or The Corkscrew. The Navajo provide guided tours and have two entrance booths with a set fee for both Lower and Upper Antelope.

Lake Powell is 10 miles from Antelope Canyon. If you're in that area, I'd highly recommend **a float trip down the Colorado River**. Our trip—a highlight for us—began right below the dam in Page, Arizona.

We took our float trip with Wilderness River Adventures, out of Lake Powell. This company also runs whitewater rafting trips out of the Grand Canyon down the Colorado River. Our trip left at about one o'clock in the afternoon. We were bused to the dam at Glen Canyon then floated on large rafts down the Colorado River for 17 miles to Lees Ferry, the beginning of the Grand Canyon.

Approximately 15 to 20 people were on each of two rafts. Matt was the guide on our boat. There, we witnessed some of the most fabulous scenery ever. The river was extremely wide and dotted here and there with fishermen. We floated deep within the canyon, and the canyon walls were fairly steep. Some of the walls were rocky with various colors and formations, and some were wooded. On this beautiful, sunny day with white cloud puffs in the sky, the water flowed swiftly, but we weren't in rapids. The raft had sides, as they all do. Although we weren't tied down, we had to wear life jackets, of course, for safety. It was a little windy and Paul's new hat blew off, but luckily our guide Matt recovered it. All in all, another perfectly beautiful day.

Website: www.riveradventures.com

Phone for reservations: 1-800-992-8022

The **all-day boat ride to Rainbow Arch from Lake Powell** was also a special experience. It looked like it might rain and possibly storm, but we decided to go anyway. We had our life jackets, rain gear, fanny packs, and extra water—everything we might need for an all-day adventure. We'd be on the Colorado River for 180 miles round trip.

The Indians say Rainbow Arch is a spiritual place, and when we got there we could feel it. We said prayers for all good things for us, the family, and the country. It seemed like the appropriate thing to do. The boat captain took us into several canyons that were so tight, we could almost touch the walls.

We were given a sack lunch, which was just okay. Overall, though, the trip was well worthwhile, especially when the weather cleared. The sky, as well as the water, was a perfect blue. Another awesome experience of beauty. Thank you, God—again.

Northwest

Victoria
Ferry
Port
Angeles
Seattle
Olympic
National
Park
Olympia
Aberdeen
Mt. St. Helens
Volcano
Longview
Columbia
River Gorge
Astoria
Seaside
Portland
Tillamook
Newport
Waldport
Yachats
Biggs
PACIFIC
OCEAN
Florence
Bend
Reedsport
Coos Bay
Crater Lake
Roseburg
Medford
Klamath Falls
OREGON
CALIFORNIA
Mt. Shasta
Eureka
Salt Lake City
Redding
San Francisco

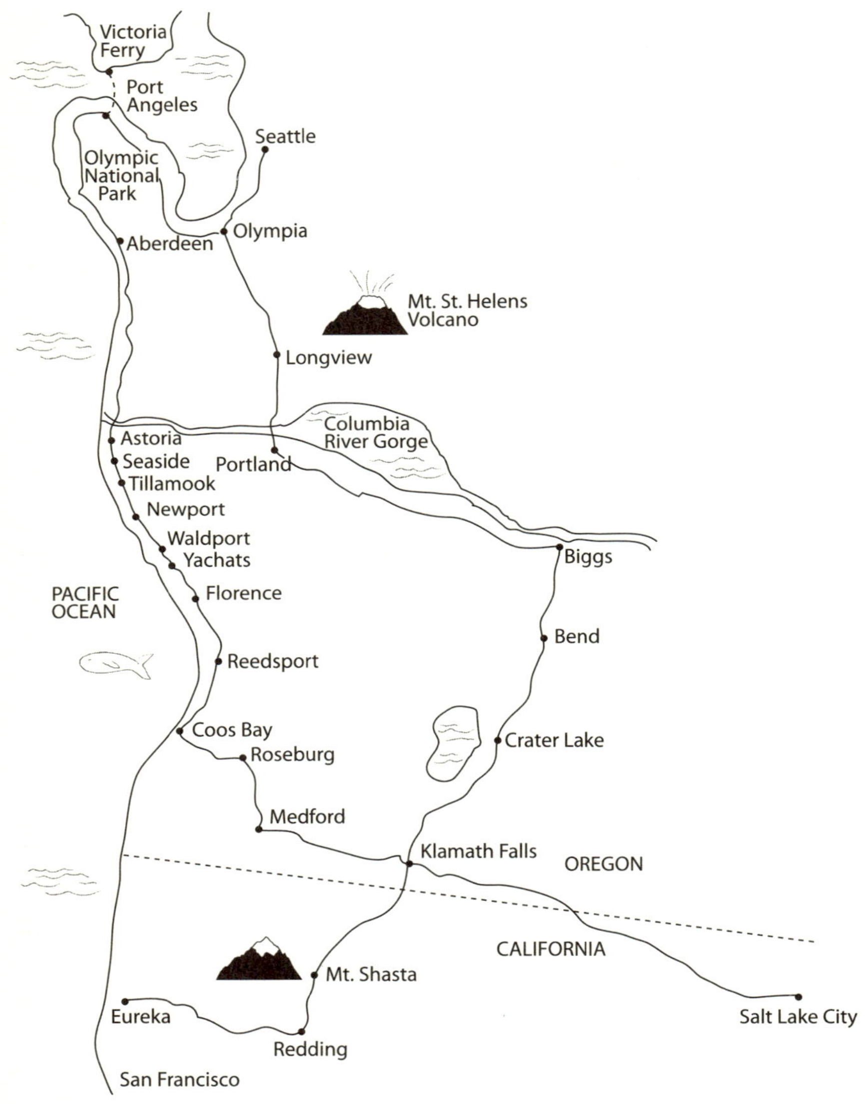

NORTHWEST

Washington State

The **Olympic National Forest** is located on the Olympic Peninsula in the northwest corner of Washington (the Evergreen State). The recreational opportunities there seem unlimited. Hiking in this lush rain forest provides a refreshing change of scenery. The large conifers and hardwoods along with emerald ferns and the moss and lichens on tree trunks and rocks make this forest a unique treat for the eyes and soul. The hiking isn't mountainous. We hiked a couple of miles.

Phone for headquarters: 360-956-2402

Mt. Rainier National Park, located 54 miles southeast of Seattle, is another great place to hike. This park is more mountainous than Olympic National Forest and has more pine trees. It isn't a rain forest, so it's not as wet. Although Mt. Rainier is a volcano, there are no signs of it being active. In fact, the mountain last erupted in1894.

Mt. St. Helens is 96 miles south of Seattle. This volcano erupted in 1980, changing the lives of thousands and transforming million of acres of pristine forest into total wasteland. Many people were warned to leave their homes before Mt. St. Helens erupted, but one man, Harry Truman, (and not the past president) refused to leave. He is buried at the base of the volcano. The trees are growing back, restoring Mt. St. Helen's beauty, and the area is educational as well. The rangers at the visitor's center describe what happened when Mt. St. Helens erupted, and we purchased an educational video of the eruption. When you hike around the mountain, ash runs over the tops of your boots.

Seattle provides many unique experiences. One of our favorite places is Pike Place Market in downtown Seattle, offering an unbelievable variety of food. It includes both a farmers' market and a seafood market as well as many kinds of restaurants for eating in or taking out. The whole place is a feast for the eyes and lots of fun. Seattle proudly celebrated Pike Place Market's 100th anniversary in 2009.

Pike Place Market: 85 Pike Street, Seattle
Phone: 206-682-7453

Oregon

Oregon has some of the most beautiful beaches in the U.S. As we traveled down the magnificent Pacific coast, we visited the following places, staying at state-operated campgrounds along the coast.

Astoria, Seaside, near the mouth of the Columbia River, was the first seaside resort in Oregon, dating back to the 1800s. The final destination of Lewis and Clark, it's both historical and filled with interesting specialty shops and art galleries. We stayed at **Astoria/Warrenton/Seaside KOA**.

Email: astoriakoa@aol.com
Phone: 503-861-2606

Cannon Beach offers many campgrounds, RV resorts, wonderful wide beaches, and a mild climate. It's a great place to relax and only 90 minutes from Portland. The campground we stayed at was **Oswald West State Park**.

Phone: 1-800-551-6949

Newport, just south of Cannon Beach, and the nearby coastal resort community of **Yachats** offer multiple opportunities for R & R, fishing, clam digging, hiking, and camping. Check out the Newport and Yachats websites for RV camping facilities.

Newport website: http://discovernewport.com

Yachats website: www.el.comto/yachats

In Newport, we stayed at **Port of Newport Marina and RV Park.**

Email: sbmarina@portofnewport.com

Phone: 541-867-3321

Portland, the City of Roses, does indeed have magnificent rose gardens. It's located on the water and sports many restaurants and specialty shops. We enjoyed walking along the waterfront with our nephew and his wife. We ate outside as the weather was in the 70s in July.

Website: www.travelportland.com/visitors

We stayed at **Portland Fairview RV Park.**

Website: www.portlandfairviewrv.com

Phone: 503-661-1047

Bend has easy access to an array of outdoor activities, including skiing, biking, whitewater rafting and kayaking, hiking, golf, and world-class fly fishing. Mount Bachelor, one of the Northwest's top ski resorts, is just 22 miles from downtown. The city is surrounded by volcanic peaks. People who live in Bend take their outdoors seriously. The city has 48 miles of in-town trails (and four microbreweries, if you'd like a cold one after your walk). Bend is a perfect place to recharge your batteries.

Crater Lake is located in south central Oregon in the Cascade Mountain Range, 100 miles east of the Pacific Ocean. It's the main feature of Crater Lake National Park and famous for its deep blue color. Few places on Earth command the overwhelming awe that Crater Lake commands from its observers. A MUST SEE! The color is a product of its great depth, the purity and clarity of its water, and the way solar radiation interacts with water. No place on earth can showcase a deep pure lake so blue in color. Crater Lake is surrounded by cliffs almost 2,000 feet high, created by its violent volcanic past, and two picturesque islands grace its waters. The entire scene is truly one of immeasurable beauty.

WEST COAST

California

Mendocino, on the spectacular California coast, offers art galleries, music, and wine tasting. It's the home of the world renowned Mendocino Music Festival, the only music festival that overlooks the Pacific Ocean. In Mendocino, you can also find a farmers' market, golfing, biking, spas, and massage therapy practitioners. As we drove up the California Coast we enjoyed the scenery and visited our friends Nell and Bill McDonald, who showed us around the Napa and Sonoma wine country. As we travel, we enjoy connecting up with family and friends.

For dates and information about the Mendocino Music Festival: 707-937-4041

Eureka is 270 miles north of San Francisco, where you'll also find spas and galleries.

San Francisco is a city beyond imagination. Restaurants, galleries, Fisherman's Wharf, plus the unique cable cars and beautiful vistas overlooking San Francisco Bay make this city a real treat. Be sure to make time to take it all in. I would suggest staying about five days in places like San Francisco. In the smaller towns, two or three days might be enough time. We stayed at a small but convenient in-town RV park in Santa Rosa and took the metro into San Francisco several days in a row to see the sights.

Mount Shasta on the north coast of California has no rival. It's home to mountaineers and other backcountry enthusiasts. Mount Shasta isn't near any other mountain. It rises abruptly and stands nearly 10,000 feet above the surrounding terrain. Because of its prominence, it casts a gigantic shadow at sunrise. Many trails wind up the mountain, and we hiked up a short distance.

Travel north from the Golden Gate Bridge in San Francisco up California Route 1 for panoramic coastal views, or take Hwy 101 for a faster route. In Humboldt County in northern California, you'll find over 100 miles of coastal redwood forest in Redwood National Park and Humboldt Redwoods State Park. Be sure to drive the Avenue of the Giants, part of Hwy 101 that winds through the state park amid the world's largest old growth redwood forest where you'll see the tallest trees in the world. The redwoods are approximately 280 miles north of San Francisco, about a five- to six-hour drive, or about 150 miles from Mount Shasta, about a three-hour drive.

The Monterey Peninsula and the towns of Monterey and Carmel are just south of the Bay Area. Monterey is a famous fishing town, and the shops along Cannery Row are unique. All the old canneries were turned into shops and restaurants. The Monterey Bay Aquarium is state of the art, and the restaurants of Fisherman's Wharf provide a special taste of the sea.

Monterey's neighbor, Carmel, boasts one of California's most expensive public beaches, Carmel Beach. The 17-mile drive along the coast is impassible after landslides or erosions or when wet, which is a lot of the time. You have to pay to drive this picturesque 17-mile stretch past the famous Pebble Beach Golf Course. However, if you patronage certain restaurants, your toll will be refunded. The town of Carmel with its one-of-a-kind upscale shops and cafés is lovely and walk-able. California Governor Arnold Schwarzenegger lives in Monterey County.

Directions: If you're traveling south on Hwy 280, take Route 17 through the Santa Cruz Mountains and connect with California Route 1 to Monterey and Carmel.

Visit both **Napa and Sonoma Valleys** to taste the best of California wines and partake of the beauty and hospitality offered. The area includes great spas with thermal baths, five-star restaurants, and inviting small towns along the way. When we were in Sonoma, our friends the McDonalds took us to some elegant wineries that were on the grounds of Chateaus. We felt as if we were in France as we sat outside looking at the rolling hills, drinking wine, and sampling hors d'oeuvres. We really enjoyed the experience and decided that Kendall Jackson was one of our favorite wines.

Yosemite National Park provides an awe-inspiring and life-changing experience. Few California vacations compare to Yosemite. Mono County is the eastern gateway to the park. Many travelers choose this approach because of the impressive views of the Eastern Sierras or because they're traveling from Death Valley, the Grand Canyon, or Nevada. Please note that Yosemite's east entrance is open dependably only from June through October due to heavy winter snows. You're advised to call ahead if in doubt.

Phone for Yosemite road conditions: 209-372-0200 (press 1 then 1)

Yosemite Valley is an hour-and-a-half drive from Lee Vining and well worth the trip. Several of the world's tallest waterfalls drop into this deep, glacier-carved, u-shaped valley, which is best seen in the early summer. The massive monoliths Half Dome, El Capitan, and Sentinel Rock are among many impressive geologic features of Yosemite Valley. Look up with binoculars to see rock climbers high on their granite faces.

Photographs of these wonders by Ansel Adams popularized Yosemite and helped establish landscape photography as an art form. The **Ansel Adams Gallery** in Yosemite Valley is a Must See for anyone who appreciates nature and fine art photography.

Note: Our friend Charles Cramer, who has won many awards for his work, has photographs displayed in the Ansel Adams Gallery. When I was in the art business, I represented Charlie. See his work at www.CharlesCramer.com.

Yosemite is one of my favorites. Don't miss it!

San Diego is relatively free of freeways. The city spreads gracefully around a curving bay. This second largest city in California is easy going with a comfortable temperature year-round. The site of the first mission in California, the city expanded quickly with the arrival of the Santa Fe Railroad in the 1880s. It's long been in the shadow of Los Angeles. However, during World War II, the U.S. Navy made San Diego its Pacific Command Center, and the Military continues to dominate the local economy along with tourism.

Places of interest to visit include: Sea World Adventure Park, the San Diego Zoo, Balboa Park, Mission Beach, Old Town, Belmont Park, and the Maritime Museum of San Diego. Belmont Park is San Diego's beachfront amusement center, just a step from surf and sand in Mission Beach. It offers everything from rides and games to shopping and oceanfront dining. Here you'll find something for the whole family. Parking and admission to the park are free.

Alaska

Prudhoe Bay
Mt. McKinley
Fairbanks
Denali
National
Park
Talkeetna
Alaska
Tok
Whitehorse
Anchorage
Glenhallen
Valdez
Haines
Junction
Yukon
Territory
Watson Lake
Yukon
Territory
Soldotna
Seward
Ferry
Skagway
Homer
Haines
British
Columbia
Muncho
Lake
Fort
Nelson
Milepost "O"
Dawson
Creek
Prince
George
Jasper
Icefields
Parkway
Medicine
Hat
Banff
Calgary
Weyburn

ALASKA AND PLACES ON THE WAY AND BACK

In July of 1999, we set out to drive to Alaska—11,000 miles round trip from St. Louis, Missouri. We were living in a 25-foot Holiday Rambler trailer being pulled by an 8-cylinder Chevy Tahoe. The trailer was the right size to allow us to get into state parks and campgrounds that could only accommodate small campers or trailers. The Tahoe had enough power to pull us up the steep inclines we'd probably encounter along the way. The trip would take us three months: one month to get to Alaska, which was four thousand miles, one month touring Alaska, and one month to get home.

Note: If you go to Alaska, don't leave home without a ***Milepost Magazine****, which tells you what to expect every milepost along the Alcon Highway.*

We started on July 15 and drove to **Madison, Wisconsin**, where we stayed at Mendota State Park off County Road M, visiting friends who'd recently moved there.

Madison is a special city. If you like cheese and beer, you'll love Madison. Wisconsin is known as the Cheese State, and Madison is the home of micro beer breweries. Madison's "Museum Mile" and beautiful state capitol building are sights to behold. The town has endless beaches, as it's located on an isthmus between Lakes Mendota and Monona within the Four Lakes region. It's also graced with beautiful parks and botanical gardens.

Madison is the home of the University of Wisconsin. It attracts a lot of entertainment, culture, and terrific night life because of the student population. Biking is a popular sport.

The excitement centers on downtown Madison. The main downtown thoroughfare is State Street, which is lined with restaurants, espresso cafes, and shops. Only pedestrians, buses, police, delivery vehicles, and bikes are allowed on State Street. Every Saturday morning the Dane County Farmers' Market is held around Capital Square. Madison is said to contain more restaurants per capita than any other American city.

Located in south central Wisconsin, Madison is 77 miles west of Milwaukee and 122 miles northwest of Chicago.

Menomonie, Wisconsin, is 177 miles from Madison. We stopped at the Twin Springs Camping Resort just minutes from I-94 on beautiful Lake Menomonie at exit 41. The peaceful campground has lots of trees. We were lucky to get a space as it fills up early.

Phone for Twin Springs: 715-235-9321

From Menomonie, we traveled 66 miles west to **Minneapolis, Minnesota**, where we visited family members and spent two nights in their driveway. Then we headed northwest 214 miles to **Fargo, North Dakota**, and from there up to **Weyburn, Saskatchewan** in Canada.

(Check your *Woodall's Campground Directory* for campgrounds. Woodall's has directories for both the U.S. and Canada.)

From Weyburn, we drove to **Medicine Hat, Alberta**, which has 2,512 hours of sunshine a year—more than any other Canadian community. It's a city of 60,000 located at the southeastern part of the Province of Alberta, Canada.

In **Calgary**, also in Alberta, we stopped at a KOA for one night. Calgary is known for its Calgary Stampede rodeo and exhibition, which takes place in July. The Stampede, which began in 1912, is a 10-day, world-class rodeo and spectacle of song and dance. During those 10 days, 500 pounds of wool are sheared, 44,000 pounds of cardboard are recycled, 32,000 flowers are planted, and 72,000 hamburgers are consumed. The event also includes a parade, and marching bands perform. Unfortunately, we were there at the wrong time of the year and missed all the festivities.

On to **Banff, Alberta**, a unique community nestled in the midst of the mountains in Canada's first national park. God's country! The mountains, lakes, countryside—all are spectacular. We just loved it, and I'm so grateful we could experience this place. The town of Banff is known as the world's finest park. Why? It has activities for every sportsman imaginable in summer and winter. It has the world's finest view, finest dining, finest spas, and finest accommodations. Therefore it's considered the world's finest park. In the winter, you can skate and both downhill and cross-country ski. Other times of the year, you can go hiking, whitewater rafting, kayaking, golfing, or fishing—not to mention shopping and dining in style. This area is called Canada's protected playground.

Lake Louise of Banff National Park is Canada's "Diamond in the Wilderness." The area of the park around Lake Louise is called the "Hiking Capital of Canada." It has one of North America's best downhill ski areas as well as hiking and walking trails, and spectacular mountain scenery.

The village of Lake Louise is on the Trans-Canada Highway, 57 kilometers or 35 miles west of Banff. It has great dining and spectacular accommodations.

Website: www.lakelouise.com

The campground was in Banff National Park of Canada.

Phone: 403-762-1550 or fax: 403-762-3380

We stayed in Lake Louise for two days and toured the famous Lake Louise Hotel and walked by the lake. There, we saw a man dressed in shorts, suspenders, and high socks blowing the Swiss horn.

Lake Moraine, in the immediate vicinity of Lake Louise, is called "the other lake." It's open in the summer only. If you want to take advantage of activities on the lake, start early. Be sure to head out before 9:30 in the morning as it can get busy. In the summer, the area is packed with tourists. The roads can be crowded with tour buses so leave early for your next destination.

The nearest town to Lake Louise is **Jasper**, three hours away and the next town en route to Alaska. In the heart of the Rocky Mountains, Jasper is the gateway to some of the most majestic accessible wilderness in Canada. As you drive the Icefields Parkway, you'll see beautiful splendor in any season. This parkway is one of the most spectacular mountain highways in the world. It takes you to Jasper from Calgary, Banff, and Lake Louise, but you can get to Jasper driving from any direction. No matter how you approach them, the Rocky Mountains become more spectacular the closer you get.

We drove up the Icefields Parkway and stopped at **Mount Robeson**, the highest mountain in the Canadian Rockies and one of the great mountains of the world. It's located in Fraser

Valley, east of the Robeson River. We continued on to Jasper where we spent the night at Whistler's Campground (877-737-3783). Jasper is 100 miles north of Lake Louise.

Athabasca Falls on Highway 93 (from Icefields Parkway just south of Jasper about 25 kilometers) is worth another stop. Parking is available just a short walk to the falls. The headwater comes from the Columbia Glacier about 70 kilometers south. Athabasca is among the most powerful and breathtaking falls in the Rocky Mountains. In winter, you can go cross-country skiing. In summer, whitewater rafting.

We drove through **Prince George** and on to **Dawson Creek** where the **Alcon Highway** begins at Mile Zero—and where the real adventure begins. If you're driving, I suggest you install rock guards and bug screens on your car or RV. Be sure to have your *Milepost Magazine* handy, as it will inform you of what to expect at every mile of the Alcon Highway.

Note: On the Alcon Highway, you might have to drive 100 miles to find a gas station, so be sure to watch your gas gauge and fill up when you can.

Fort Nelson was our next stop, about 300 miles from Dawson Creek. It's a major town and stopover destination for travelers leaving British Columbia for the Yukon and beyond. Fort Nelson sits as the gateway to the immense wilderness of the Rocky Mountains, the Yukon, Northwest Territories, and Alaska. You'll notice wildlife as you travel through this area. We didn't stay at Fort Nelson but traveled on to Muncho Lake.

Muncho Lake in northern British Columbia is a Must Stop, Must See place. The lake area has a perpetually blue hue, which results from copper oxide leaching out of the bedrock. Hwy 97 follows the east side of Muncho Lake and passes beside both **Strawberry Flats Campground** and **MacDonald Campground**. The MacDonald Campground has its own boat launch, and we stayed there because it's in the middle of the Muncho Lake area.

For campsite reservations: 1-800-689-9025

For Canada Parks: 1-877-reserve

We launched our boat, the Sea Eagle, on Muncho Lake. It's an inflatable boat about 12 feet by 3 feet that can hold two adults and a child. It can be inflated with a pump and has wooden floorboards. When deflated, it fits into a bag—just the right size to fit into a car or RV. We have a 3.3 horsepower motor to hang on the back of the Sea Eagle that we conveniently keep in the back of the Tahoe. We've used our boat on many lakes as we travel.

Note: Besides hiking up trails, one of the best ways to appreciate the mountains is to get out on the lake in a boat so you can get a full view.

At **Watson Lake in the Yukon**, we stayed at an in-town campground called **Watson Lake Campground**. We were able to see an interesting and informative film about the Aurora Borealis at the Northern Lights Theater and enjoyed delicious halibut and lamb chops at the Belvedere Hotel.

At Watson Lake is found the **Sign Post Forest**. Here's the fun story behind this phenomenon: During World War II, an emergency project was launched to connect Alaska to southern Canada by road. This unpaved road, known as the Alaska Highway, eventually ran 1,500 miles from Dawson Creek, British Columbia, to Fairbanks, Alaska. While working on the Alaska Highway, a homesick U.S. Army GI named Carl K. Lindley erected a sign pointing the way and stating mileage to his home town of Danville, Illinois. This is how the Sign Post Forest began. Over the years, people have made and brought signs from all over the world and country to display here, and at last count in 1999, the Forest was home to 30,000 signs. We made our sign for St. Louis, Missouri, as we traveled and added it to the Forest on the way back home.

Website: www.yukoninfo.comwatson/signpostforest.htm

Whitehorse, Yukon, was our next stop, 263 miles northwest of Watson Lake. Whitehorse, the capital of the Yukon since 1953, was established as a riverboat hub in the 1890s. The Klondike Gold Rush Railway arrived in 1902, and the U.S. Army brought the Alaska Highway to town in 1940. Whitehorse offers many festivals, hot springs, and museums—and dog sledding as well. You might want to catch the Frantic Follies, a fun vaudeville revue.

We stayed at **Hi Country RV**, the most popular RV Park in Whitehorse. It's by the Alaska Highway, three minutes out of downtown.

Phone for reservations: 867-667-7445

Note: In Alaska and Canada, you can rent a cab RV fully equipped with linens and sheets through Cruise America.com. That way, if you don't have the time to spend getting there, you can see Alaska in about two weeks.

Miles Canyon holds the rapids on the Yukon River where Gold Rushers had to transport their 2,000 pounds of supplies.

Originally referred to as Grand Canyon, it was renamed in 1883 after General Nelson Miles. The ferocity of the rapids made them very dangerous during the Gold Rush. Hundreds of boats loaded with supplies and lives were lost trying to navigate them. Eventually the rail system around the canyon eliminated this hazard. Then the North West Mounted Police regulated traffic.

We traveled on through **Carcross**, which got its name from combining Caribou Crossing. We settled for three days in **Skagway**. Our campground was right next to the ferry, near where cruise ships come in to dock. Being a cruise ship port, Skagway is a bustling town. The sites were tight, but the campground was in a great location because we could walk everywhere. During the Klondike Gold Rush, Skagway was the gateway to Canada and the Yukon River system for most of the adventurers who traveled north to seek their fortunes. The town still capitalizes on the 1898 stampede, but now is a tourist center with an outstanding heritage. Skagway can be reached by road or from the sea.

In Skagway, Paul bought me a beautiful 14K gold eagle—just what I wanted. It's surrounded by gold nuggets and quite unique. My honey provided me with my own Gold Rush!

The Chilkoot Trail is one of two main routes to the Klondike that were established long before the Gold Rush. It covers 33 miles and is accessible only by foot, taking three to five days to cover the distance. The trail begins at the Taiya River bridge near Dyea, the ghost town that was the starting point of the Chilkoot Trail during the Gold Rush, and continues over the Chilkoot Pass to Lake Bennett.

Note: Interestingly, no gold was ever found in Skagway River Valley. The actual gold field was 550 miles north near the junction of the Klondike and Yukon Rivers in Dawson City. Skagway became a bustling supply town known as the gateway to the Klondike gold field.

We rode the railway from Skagway to White Pass, traveling the Yukon route taken by the Gold Rushers. The railway is a narrow gauge that's been rebuilt and looks like it did in 1898. We chugged along Dead Horse Pass through mountains and over streams. What a beautiful three-and-a-half-hour ride—a great trip! Many tours leave from Skagway, and some include dog sledding.

From Skagway, we took the car ferry to **Haines**. The ferry took only an hour and was an easy ride. Not as commercial as Skagway, Haines is surrounded by abundant wildlife and endless opportunities for outdoor adventures such as hunting and fishing. Located on the shores of Lynn Canal, Haines is home to the first permanent U.S. Army post in Alaska and also to the Chilkot natives.

Note: The Haines Highway into Canada was previously the Dalton trail used by Gold Rushers. The Tlingit Indian trade route to the interior was dubbed the "grease trail" because an important item carried via that route was oil extracted from the eulachon fish. Resources abound in this area.

We passed an eagle preserve on our way out of Haines, but we saw only one eagle. The time to see thousands of eagles is November, when Haines has its Alaskan Bald Eagle Festival.

Website: www.haines.ak.us/index.php

We stopped at **Cottonwood Park Campground on Kluane Lake**. It's just 17 miles south of **Destruction Bay** and 150 miles west of Whitehorse on the Alaskan Highway. We thought Destruction Bay in the Yukon was one of the most beautiful spots on our trip. The campground overlooks the crystal clear lake and provides an excellent place to stop and catch your breath. The friendly owners made it one of our favorite settings for a campground.

Email for Cottonwood Park Campground: glen.brough@sympatico.ca

Phone: 867-841-4066

Next stop was **Tok**, known as the Gateway to Alaska. We stayed at the **Tok RV Village**. It's a good campground within walking distance to the visitor center and the Salmon Bake.

Phone: 907-883-5877

Toll free inside Canada: 1-800-478-5878

Email: camp@tokrv.net

We drove to **Liberty Falls** down the Richardson Highway on the way to **Valdez**. Liberty Falls is a beautiful natural falls with a remote campground that has no services. It has only three sites, all offering just the kind of peacefulness we like.

We drove down a dirt road toward **McCarthy**. It followed the tracks of the railroad in 1898. **Kennecott** is also up by McCarthy. These are two ghost towns. Kennecott had a famous copper mine, which is now closed. The road was so rough that after a few miles we decided to turn back. On our way to McCarthy, we stopped at **Chitina** for gas and groceries. The grocery store was unbelievable. On the outside, it appeared to be no more than a shack, but on the inside, had everything one could possibly imagine.

We stayed at **Squirrel Creek State Recreational Site**, located near Glennallen in the Copper Valley on the Richardson Highway. When we left, it was rainy and cold, but as Paul's dad had told us, the rain always stops by noon, and it did just that.

As we drove into **Valdez**, called the "Little Switzerland of Alaska," the fog began to lift. We were met with more beauty than ever—spectacular mountains, waterfalls, glaciers, and streams. We took a helicopter ride with Stan, a highly experienced pilot, to see these sights from the air. We landed on a glacier for a while. Such fun!! Stan was from Mississippi, living up in Alaska for the summer. His knowledge and interesting storytelling made the hour "fly by."

In Valdez, we went to a movie about the Alaska Pipeline that we found to be educational. Valdez is a small but very beautiful town. We took a catamaran cruise on Prince William Sound. The puffins were flying alongside the catamaran, which we found amusing. We had to buy our own toy puffin whose wings flutter when the wind blows. We still enjoy it to this day.

We took a helicopter ride over the glaciers. The view in Valdez is gorgeous. In every direction, the mountains rise into the air. No wonder they call Valdez "Alaska's Little Switzerland." The residential area is located in a quiet area of Valdez with many great trees and lush ground cover and water can be seen from most of the homes, too.

Paul and I concluded we'd never been so happy. This trip to Alaska has brought us closer together. We depend on each other, and being away from our usual responsibilities has been wonderful. The opportunity to see God's country has truly been a gift.

We left Squirrel Creek and drove to Palmer. We stopped at a drive-by espresso shack in the middle of nowhere. Very clever, these Alaskans.

We met up with friends of ours, Perry and Linda, in **Anchorage**. They played golf with us at the Anchorage Municipal Golf course on O'Mally Road. If you like golf, I'd recommend this beautiful course. That day, the weather was in the 70s—perfect for golfing.

We also took in Mr. Whitekeys' Fly By Night Club for a little comedy and never laughed so hard in our lives! Unfortunately, the club is now closed. Mr. Whitekeys has taken his show on the Alaskan road and now calls it The Whale Fat Follies. Anchorage is a big town, and by the time all was said and done, we felt as if we'd seen the best entertainment in Anchorage, and we enjoyed what we saw of the city, too.

Then we all drove from Anchorage to **Talkeetna in South Denali Park**, located 115 miles north of Anchorage, 14 miles off Parks Highway at the end of Talkeetna Spur Road. This small community of fewer than 500 people is thought to be the inspiration behind the TV series *Northern Exposure*. It's also where climbers gather who are preparing to climb Mt. McKinley.

You can reach Talkeetna by rental car or bus line to and from Denali Park, Anchorage, and Seward. The Alaskan Railroad offers summer service to Talkeetna from Anchorage, Denali Park, and Fairbanks.

In Talkeetna, Perry and Linda stayed in the B & B, and we stayed in our RV in the parking lot outside. We asked permission of the B & B owner, of course. When we woke up the first morning to a clear sky, the owner of the B & B suggested we charter a small plane and see Mt. McKinley because clear days there are few and far between. She called one of her friends who was a pilot and arranged the trip for us. We took advantage of the weather and circled Mt. McKinley for over one and a half hours. Lucky timing; the pilot said most times the mountain is covered with clouds. It was well worth the time, money, and effort. What an incredible adventure.

After our friends left, we drove to the **Kenai Peninsula**, 150 miles south of Anchorage. Kenai, known as the Alaskan Playground, includes 15,000 square miles of extraordinary adventure. For example, you can take boat trips to fish for King salmon and/or halibut. We stopped at a full hookup RV park right on the water at the Cook Inlet. The park was Beluga Lookout Lodge located at the mouth of the Kenai River and Cook Inlet. It was just beautiful.

Website: www.belugalookout.com

Phone: 1-800-745-5999

From there, we drove to **Captain Cook State Park.** This park is virtually undiscovered by most visitors to the Kenai Peninsula. It offers a peaceful setting of forests, lakes, streams, and salt water beaches. You can reach it by driving 25 miles north of Kenai on the North Kenai Road to milepost 36. You can fish for rainbow trout and silver salmon, and you may see wildlife such as moose, bear, wolves, Beluga whales, and bald eagles. The park was named for Captain James Cook, the famous English mariner, who explored what is now known as Cook Inlet in 1778.

We didn't stay there but moved on to **Soldotna**, the central hub of the Kenai Peninsula where we picked up some smoked halibut and salmon. Soldotna is home to moose, caribou, brown and black bear, wolves, dall sheep, mountain goats, eagles, swans, duck, geese, other varieties of birds, and fish. Moose often wonder into town and bald eagles are commonly seen.

Homer is one of our favorite places we've ever been. If you do go to Alaska, Homer is a Must See. We stayed at the **Land's End RV Park on the Homer Spit**. It's a breathtaking spot surrounded by the Cook Inlet and mountains. The Homer Spit protrudes into Kachemak Bay. A paved path stretches most of the four miles of the spit and is great for biking or walking. This little bit of paradise has a commercial fishing business, restaurants, hotels, sea kayaking, outfitters, art galleries, and on-the-beach camping sites. It's a great place to fly a kite, walk the beaches, and fish. **Land's End Resort** is the only beachfront hotel and has a spectacular location at the very tip of the Homer Spit.

Homer is a place where actors and artists come to perform for the summer. We saw "Taming of the Shrew" in a Quonset hut theater. They told us to go to the bathroom before we went in as the hut had no facilities and to wear a coat because it had no heat. The play was great fun and a memorable experience. Homer is considered "The Riviera of Alaska."

Phone for the Land's End RV Park: 907-235-0404

The Bear RV Park five miles outside of Seward was our next stop. We took a Kenai Fjord boat cruise, and one of the hostesses on board started chatting with us. She said what she likes most about Alaska is that "people are very accepting of everyone." Unconditional acceptance—what a beautiful world up here! I never want to forget what we came to Alaska to learn.

Phone for **Bear RV Park** reservations: 907-224-5725

The **Exit Glacier** area in **Kenai Fjords National Park** near **Seward** was a great place to hike. Only part of the park is accessible by road. You can stroll trails, walk close to an active glacier, or take a ranger-led walk. You can witness up close how glaciers reshape a landscape and learn how plant life reclaims the barren, rocky land exposed by a glacier retreat.

Directions to Exit Glacier: Turn onto the Herman Leier/ Exit Glacier Road at mile 3 off the Seward Hwy. The 8.6-mile road to the Exit Glacier area is paved and easily accessible to all types of vehicles. Taxi/shuttle is available from Seward. The Glacier is open year-round. Be sure to check current conditions before going. Exit Glacier has a 12-site "walk-in" campground, which means first come first serve. Usually they don't take reservations.

We spent the night in Talkeetna again, about 149 miles south of Denali National Park, and ate a delicious dinner at the Talkeetna Lodge. Then we headed for the park.

Denali National Park is 50 to 60 miles across. We got the last campsite at the **Savage River Campground**, which wasn't allowing any tents or soft-side campers due to the bear problem. Rangers had issued a bear warning in the park, but we took a walk anyway. Luckily, no bears. While we were in the park, we went to a fascinating dog sled presentation.

Phone for the Savage River Campground: 1-877-2Denali

When we left Denali, we headed north to **Fairbanks** and stayed at **The River's Edge** campground, which offered many amenities including river fishing because it's on the **Chena River**. The campground has its own restaurant and is close to shopping. It provides free shuttle service to Riverboat Discovery, along with tour information and ticket sales.

Website: www.rv-park-alaska.com

Phone: 907-474-0286 or 1-800-770-3343 for reservations

In Fairbanks, we visited the **University of Alaska Museum**, which displayed the full of history of Alaska. We were impressed by the history of the native Alaskan tribes, the Tlingits and the Inuits. Fairbanks is a fairly small town compared to Anchorage, and we weren't that impressed with the town itself. We did go to the Follies, though, and found that amusing.

It was in Fairbanks that we heard the geese flying overhead going south for the winter, and we decided it was time for us to head south, also.

We left Fairbanks and drove 300 miles to the Yukon. We camped at a beautiful park by Sage Creek and were lucky to get a site overlooking a lake—our favorite type of campsite. We could see reflections of the mountains in the lake. The setting looked like a postcard.

We then drove about 300 miles back to **Whitehorse** and camped at **Marsh Lake** (28 miles east of Whitehorse). The next day we were off to Watson Lake. This time through, Paul had our sign all ready for the Sign Forest. We had painted the sign in green on a natural wooden board. It looked great among the other signs.

Headed back toward St. Louis, we made it to **Muncho Lake**, British Columbia, where we'd stopped on our way up to Alaska. This place is without a doubt one of the most beautiful places on Earth and one of our favorite places on this trip.

Muncho Lake is where we smelled our brakes burning—the story I told earlier in this book. We drove to Fort Nelson then to Dawson Creek to find a place we could get them fixed.

As mentioned before, we stayed at **Tubby's RV**, which has 97 full service sites with 30 amp electric. It's located one and a half blocks east of the Alaska/Hart Highway.

Luckily, the Chevy dealer in Dawson Creek was able to repair the car and it was all under warranty. What a break—or should I say brake!

Phone for Tubby's: 250-782-2584

Onward to **Edmonton, Alberta**. We stopped at **Glowing Embers RV Park**, northwest of Edmonton on Highway 43.

Website: www.glowingembersRVpark.com

Phone: 780-962-8100

While in Edmonton, we wanted to be sure to see the **Edmonton Mall**, touted as the largest mall in the world. Its amusement park includes an aquarium for dolphins and a swimming pool with slides. We'd never seen anything like it. Although we were startled by its size and activities, visiting malls aren't the reason we travel.

We traveled on to **Glacier National Park** at **Waterton** on the Canadian side with its mountainous terrain, unparalleled scenery, and abundant wildlife. These wonders of nature greeted Lewis and Clark as they made their way through this area in 1805 in what became the U.S. area of the park. Glacier National Park includes parts of Alberta and British Columbia, Canada, and continues into Montana in the United States.

We packed a lunch, launched our boat, the Sea Eagle, and spent several hours cruising on **Waterton Lake**. The water was a beautiful navy blue and the sky was clear except for little puffs of white clouds. It was a perfect day in every way.

Onward we drove and arrived at St. Mary's at the entrance to **Glacier National Park in Montana** on the U.S. side of the border. We then traveled to the southwest entrance where we stayed at **Apgar Campground** at the end of Lake McDonald—a perfect spot. We felt as if we were living in the woods with trees all around us. Apgar has 196 campsites, which were spotless and within walking distance to the lake.

Note: Black bears can break into cars. Please store any food you have with you in anti-bear lockers provided at each campsite.

We did a bit of side-tripping and found **Polebridge** on the northwestern edge of Glacier. It's an isolated community that primarily consists of Polebridge Mercantile and Northern Lights Saloon. The roads were very challenging, but we continued farther north to **Bowman Lake**—seven to eight miles of horrible roads. The lake is gorgeous, and the town reminded us of Talkeetna. In both towns, people do their own thing and you'll find unique venues. At any time of day, you can hear people playing music. You might see people sitting outside eating delicious baked goods made at the local bakery or children playing with hula hoops. People spontaneously do whatever pleases them and everyone is most friendly.

Although the ride was rough, the scenery was well worth it. If you're interested in checking out the area, be aware that you can hike, fish, and camp.

Kalispell, Montana, is located in the perfect geographic location for visitors and residents to take advantage of a wide variety of activities. More than 2,000 artists and crafts people reside in the area. In fact, there are more bronze casting foundries here than anywhere else in the nation. On another note, Kalispell is also home to the Glacier Symphony and Chorale.

We drove on to **Gardiner** at the entrance to the North Gate of **Yellowstone National Park**. Next, we drove to **Mammoth** then stopped at **Madison Campground**, making sure to visit Old Faithful and check out the geysers. If you go, don't miss the Upper and Lower Falls, Yellowstone Lake, and the Yellowstone River, which runs through the whole landscape. The **Grand Canyon of the Yellowstone National Park** has been voted the best backpacking park area in America by *Backpacker Magazine*. What a spectacular place!

In Yellowstone, you can go boating, camping, and hiking. If you have young children in your party, they can become Junior Rangers.

Website: www.nps.gov/yell/index.htm

We were leaving Yellowstone the next day and had to get up very early as the East Gate is open only from 6 a.m. to 10 a.m. and then again in the evening. We had quite a distance to travel to get there in time. They closed the road in the middle of the day because of construction work on the road. We were almost at the East Gate when we came across a huge buffalo standing in the middle of the road. He didn't seem at all interested in moving. As we slowly approached him, he just stood there. We felt like getting out of the car and giving him a push, but considering his size, we thought better of it. Finally, after what seemed like forever (but probably only five or ten minutes), he sauntered on across the road. Luckily, we made the gate in time, but it was a close call.

Cody, Wyoming, was another favorite stop. **The Buffalo Bill Museum** is a treat. Buffalo Bill led quite a colorful life, as depicted in the museum. The museum houses a fabulous art collection, gun collection, and the history of Buffalo Bill's horse shows. Educational and definitely worth a visit.

We spent the night in **Shell, Wyoming** at the **Shell Campground**, 1021 First Street; phone 307-765-9924.

After leaving Shell, we had to drive though the **Big Horn Mountains**—beautiful scenery but very challenging for Paul and "Big Red," our Tahoe pulling our trailer. We climbed to about 9,000 feet, then on the downgrade, we experienced fierce wind and had to go slow. When we got on the interstate, we picked up time and made it across Wyoming to Spearfish, South Dakota.

The **Badlands National Park in South Dakota** contains the world's richest Oligocene Epoch fossil beds, dating back 33.7 to 23.8 million years. The evolutionary stories of mammals such as the horse and rhinoceros are told in these 244,000 acres of sharply eroded buttes, pinnacles, and spires. Bison, big horn sheep, endangered black-footed ferrets, and swift fox roam one of the largest protected mixed grass prairies in the U.S.

The climate in the Badlands is variable and unpredictable, from minus 40 degrees in the winter to a scorching 116 degrees in the hot, dry summers. In winters, they get between 12 and 24 inches of snow. High winds blow across the land year round.

Note: While in the Badlands, dress in layers, wear a hat, and use sunscreen. Hydrate well, especially if you're hiking.

Wall Drug on the northeastern edge of the South Dakota Badlands was established in December, 1931. In this legendary store, you'll find souvenirs, toy guns, t-shirts, and everything else imaginable. If you "must have" a pair of western spurs, you can probably find any kind you like there. Don't miss Wall Drug. It's an icon of tradition in South Dakota. As you travel toward it, signs give you the miles to Wall Drug. Other fun signs we saw on our way were "Free Water at Wall Drug" (a big thing in the stagecoach days!) and "As seen in the N.Y. Times" or "As seen in the Washington Post." Some signs listed "everything" that Wall Drug sold.

Mitchell, South Dakota, was incorporated in 1881 and named for banker Alexander Mitchell, president of the Chicago, Milwaukee, and St. Paul Railroad. Mitchell's biggest claim to fame, though, is the **Corn Palace**. Decorated in murals made of several colors of dried corn and grains, the theme of the Corn Palace changes annually. The building is used for concerts, circuses, high school proms, graduations, and trade shows. Mitchell also boasts a prehistoric Indian village. Visit this historic city and step back in time. You won't be sorry.

Alaska was an unbelievable trip of a lifetime, a never-to-be-forgotten experience. It changed my outlook on life. We met the most helpful people along the way. As we traveled, we felt so lucky to have this chance to see such spectacular country. My wish is for you, too, to experience such a magnificent slice of life.

EASTERN CANADA

Further adventures took us back into Canada—this time to the east, where we enjoyed parts of Ontario, Newfoundland, Nova Scotia, and Prince Edward Island, and traveled up the St. Lawrence Seaway to fulfill a childhood dream of Paul's.

Ontario

On this trip, we drove north on Hwy 94 in Michigan heading to Hwy 69, which took us to our border crossing at Port Huron on the Michigan side and Sarnia on the Ontario side.

At **Stratford, Ontario**, we stayed at the Wildwood Conservation Area of the Upper Thames River Conservation Authority. I found this to be one of the best spots to camp and one of the most beautiful cities to visit. We love the theater, and we greatly enjoyed the many theater productions at the three theaters in Stratford. The weather is ideal in the summer, with the temperature in the 70s in August. The quaint town of Stratford with the Thames River running through it reminds me of England. I give Stratford a four-star rating—one of our most memorable vacation spots.

The Shakespeare Festival in Stratford is at the top of my list! If you love theater, it's the place for you. The theaters present topnotch performances, and not all Shakespeare. We saw Oklahoma! and several other plays. Stratford is a great getaway, especially if you live in a climate that's too hot in the summer and want a break. The town offers great shopping, excellent restaurants, and—my husband's favorite—golf.

The **Wildwood Conservation Area campground** is about five minutes from St. Mary's and about 10 to15 minutes from Stratford. The park offers accommodations for tents as well as campers and has a wonderful lake for boating, a sports field, a pool, and a playground for children. It's quiet and has lots of trees.

Phone for reservations: 866-668-2267

Just a short distance from Stratford and about five miles from the city of Goderich, we stayed at **Shelter Valley**—a campground we give at least four stars. Its benefits include many activities for children and a river, if you like to fish or just watch it flow by.

Email: shelter.valley@explornet.com

Goderich is a town of about 42,000 people built around a hub with streets coming out like spokes. The library is unique, with turrets, detailed woodwork, and paneled doors. Goderich is the prettiest town in Ontario—at least according to Bert, one of the owners of the campground. Located on the shores of Lake Huron, the town has lovely beaches where we brought our beach chairs and lunch almost every day. A boardwalk meanders along the lake, further enhancing the town's picturesque nature.

About 50 miles north of Goderich, we explored **Kincardine** with its stunning quaint homes.

Newfoundland

Newfoundland is rugged and mountainous. Canadian Hwy 1, which connects most major cities in Canada, is in excellent shape. The famous Canadian national park **Gros Morne** (meaning large mountain) offers spectacular mountain and seascape views. Exquisite, clear waters cut through the mountains. The city of **Rocky Harbor** is a good location if you want to spend some time in the park.

Website: www.grosmorne.com

The ferry to the town of **Channel-Port aux Basques** is the largest car ferry in the world and provided a pleasant five-hour ride. The gift shops and places to eat on the ferry made the time go by quickly! Another car ferry (15-hour ride) will take you to the capital city of St. John on the other side of the island.

Nova Scotia

We recommend **Campground Lakeview Treasure** right on Highway 22 a short distance from the town of Louisbourg and 20 minutes from Sydney, a much larger city.

Phone for campground reservation: 902-733-2058

The **Fortress of Louisbourg** is a Canadian National Park Historic Site. Don't miss this attraction. Completely restored in the past 40 years, it's a replica of the original fortress where the battles between the English and the French took place in the 1700s and 1800s. The Fortress is authentic down to the soldiers' dress and muskets, and the women's and children's dress. The two restaurants serve the same food that was served in the 1800s. The dishes are porcelain and pewter. We had fish and vegetables, and apple pie with whipped cream for dessert. Everything was delicious!

The furniture is all period and you really feel as though you're back in the 1800s. Many buildings made up the community. The barracks where the soldiers lived were being restored when we visited. This unique place definitely provides a step back in time, an immersion in history. August weather is in the 60s and 70s.

http://www.louisbourg.ca/fort/

The scenery and rugged rocks that meet the ocean in the **Cape Breton Highlands National Park** are unbelievable. The **Cabot Trail** follows the coastline, and much of the trail is in the park. Going north, it parallels the Atlantic Ocean to the east. Then it crosses the mountains and heads south, winding along beside the Gulf of St. Lawrence on the west.

In **Ingonish, Nova Scotia**, we stayed at the beautiful **Keltic Lodge**. A four-course dinner and buffet breakfast was included in the overnight stay. Hiking trails provide a breathtaking view of the ocean. I give the Keltic Lodge a five-star rating. To top it off, the place offers an 18-hole golf course, which really pleased Paul.

Phone: 1-800-565-0444

Prince Edward Island (PEI)

We drove across the bridge to **Prince Edward Island** on Hwy 1, also called the Trans-Canada Highway. We stayed at the family-owned Sun-N-Shade Campground just across the bridge, which has large, grassy sites. The owners are musicians and they regularly get together with other musicians living on the island. At the campground, they entertained everyone playing all kinds of music. They invited the audience to dance, and one couple took them up on it.

Sun-N-Shade email: info@sun-n-shade.com

Phone: 902-855-3492 or Fax: 902-855-2094

Tourism information for PEI: 1-800-463-4PEI

Charlottetown, the largest city on PEI and its capital, has great biking trails. Outdoor cafés and restaurants are found at Victoria Row as well as numerous gift shops. The Confederate Centre has an art gallery and often presents plays.

Cavendish is where Lucy Montgomery lived and wrote the book *Anne of Green Gables.* When you visit Lucy Montgomery's house, which is preserved for visitors, you'll see Cavendish through Lucy's eyes. You can walk the beach, play golf, or go deep sea fishing. Music festivals are also popular in Cavendish.

The Prince Edward Island National Park borders on the beaches, which are something to see with their magnificent sand dunes. You'll find plenty of hiking trails and campgrounds.

Dalvay by the Sea is located east of Charlottetown. This elegant Victorian structure was built in 1896 by an American industrialist. It's now an inn with 26 guest rooms, eight cottages, and a restaurant. *Fodor's Travel Guide* comments that it's "one of Canada's great country inns." Lobster, scallops, shrimp, and mussels are specialties in this area. Dalvay by the Sea was designated a National Historic Site in 1994 because of its architectural significance.

The St. Lawrence Seaway

My husband, Paul, always dreamed of going to the Gaspé Peninsula and driving up the St. Lawrence Seaway to the sea. When he was a little boy, he read the book *Paddle to the Sea* about an Indian boy living near Lake Superior. He carved and painted a little wooden boat paddled by a wooden Indian he named Paddle to the Sea. Then he carved the words "Paddle to the Sea" on the boat so anyone who found "Paddle" would put him back in the water. He set the boat on a bank of snow. When the snow melted in the spring, the boat was carried into Lake Superior and traveled all through the Great Lakes. People rescued Paddle to the Sea whenever he got stuck someplace and sent him on his way again.

This book—Paul's favorite as a child—inspired him to follow the St. Lawrence River to the sea, and that's exactly what we did. As it was with Paddle, people we met along the way gave us tips and sent us on our way. There seems to be a coincidental parallel. As I always say, there are no accidents, only coincidences.

We felt so grateful to be able to see this part of our world. Can you tell that gratitude has been a major theme throughout all our travels? We feel so blessed!

All in All

Why did I write this book? For several reasons.

First, many of the readers of my first book have been asking me to write another one. I felt I had a lot more to share and owed it to them to continue our story.

Second, my husband, Paul, and I have had so much fun and learned so many things about this great land we live in that I wanted to share our travels and our fun with you.

I hope all of you who have the desire to travel will find this book helpful. May you have great experiences, meet fantastic people, and have a ton of fun.

Remember, life is short—don't wait.

Anita Henehan

Things We Learned the Hard Way

- Put a checklist by the door to the coach or trailer of all essential things to do.
- Go over the RV, check the mechanical parts, and make any needed repairs before you leave on a trip.
- In particular, check the turn signals and brake lights on the tow car.
- Check the pins and the electric plug-in on the tow bar.
- Make sure you know how to hook up the car to the motor coach.
- Always remember to put the tow vehicle in towing mode so you won't ruin the transmission.
- Before you leave from anywhere, make sure everything in the motor home is put away, the cabinets and drawers are closed, and the shower door is locked.
- Make sure everything is inside the coach before you take off. The hose and the electric cord should be in the rig; the step should be up; the antenna should be down; your wife should be in the rig.
- Know how to jumpstart a car if the battery dies.
- Check the air pressure in all the tires in the coach and the tow car before leaving anywhere. It's hard to notice the tow vehicle's tires when you're driving the coach.

- Before pulling away, make sure slide-outs are brought in—easy to forget.
- Before extending the slide-out, check the surroundings for trees, rocks, guard rails, water faucets, and small children. (One of our friends was extending the slide-out and it hit a guard rail. The man repairing the coach said this is more common than you'd think.)
- When you're dumping, don't open the black valve all the way. Ease the valve open and let it start flowing. Once you're sure everything is okay, then open the valve all the way. (In a messy situation, as we opened the black valve, the black water rushed out through the hose, which had many pinholes in it from wear. You can imagine what a mess we had.)
- Don't forget the RV manual; you never know when you might need it.
- Keep a flashlight next to the bed at night. That way, if you lose power or have an emergency after dark, you don't have to search for one.
- Likewise, keep your cell phone by the side of your bed . . .
- And keep your car keys nearby to set off the car alarm if it becomes necessary.
- Take a waterproof safe with important information such as passports and titles to your vehicles. One couple wanted to sell their coach while traveling but didn't have the title with them.

- Take plenty of extra blankets; you can never predict the weather.
- Take a phone list of most-called numbers.
- Heed advice from our friends who were campground hosts in Missouri State Parks and have numbers for park rangers and others to call for backup, if needed.
- If you're a campground hosts, get trained in first aid and CPR—beneficial skills to have.
- If you hear barking as you pull out, you've probably forgotten the dog.
- Don't travel in hail if you can avoid it. Hail can heavily damage your coach and car. Be aware of weather reports and advisories.
- If you're towing a car with all four wheels on the ground, make sure that any time you turn in to a place (such as a restaurant), you can pull straight out when you leave. Backing out is impossible with a tow car. You'd have to unhook it.
- When you're pulling out of a parking lot in a motor coach, be sure to pull straight out. The coach will flex, but the windshield will not. (We were in Los Cruses, New Mexico, and pulled out of the RV dealer's lot at an angle. Several miles down the highway, we discovered the windshield on the driver's side had separated from the coach. Back to the RV dealer for repairs!)

- If the weather report predicts the temperature will fall below freezing, unhook your water hose from the water main or your hose will freeze solid.
- If it's rainy or windy, be sure to put the awning up. Our friends had water pull the awning down and they couldn't get out of their trailer.
- If you're staying in one place for a long time, start the engine and move the coach forward and backward periodically—about once a month. If you do this, the tires won't wear out, as they otherwise will when the coach sits in one place.
- Don't be afraid to ask others for help if you're having a problem.
- When you get to a new place, take a trolley tour of the city to get oriented (if available); alternatively, go to the visitor center to find out the best places to see and to eat, and always get to know the locals.
- We learned it's important to have PATIENCE. When we were in Bend, Oregon, the Aqua Hot (our heating system) quit working. We had to wait two days for the parts to be shipped to us to repair the problem.
- Perhaps the most important—don't forget to take your SENSE OF HUMOR. You'll need it more often than you can imagine!

Things That Are Good to Know

- RVers are allowed to spend the night in Flying J, Cracker Barrel, and Walmart parking lots, if necessary. Be sure to ask the manager first if it's alright to spend the night. We use Walmart parking lots often and have friends who've stayed in Cracker Barrel parking lots overnight. Each Cracker Barrel has maps of every location in the U.S., and you can purchase an atlas at Walmart giving you a list of the Walmarts all over the country. It seems safe to park in their lots.
- Stop and find a place to stay way before dark. When you arrive at a reasonable hour, you can get set up, take a walk, and relax before dinner. If a problem arises, it's usually easier to fix before nightfall.
- A cell phone can be indispensible to call ahead for reservations or in case of emergency. Don't forget your cell phone charger.
- Try staying in one place for four to five days so you can get to know the area. Extended stays can be educational as well as relaxing.
- It may seem obvious, but always carry insurance and keep your card and information with you. We use RV Alliance America insurance. Call toll free 1-800-521-2942 or log on to www.rvaa.com.

- Maintenance and Repair: REC-TEC RV & Trailer Services, St. Louis, MO, if you're in the area. Phone: 314-731-9080
- Prepare for any kind of weather when out and about; it can change in a flash.
- After or during a heavy rain, don't park on grass or dirt if you can help it.
- Take a map not only when you're driving but when you're hiking trails.
- For information about recreational sites all around the U.S., see: www.recreation.gov
- For information about U.S. state parks, see: www.stateparks.com/usa.html
- A Golden Age Passport (purchased at National Parks and Corp of Engineer Parks) entitles two people to camp in these national parks for half price. Admission to the parks is free. Cost for the Passport is $10.00 for life. For details: www.nps.gov
- Consult the *Woodall's Campground Directory* series for the U.S. and Canada. You can purchase these directories at Camping World all over the U.S. or at www.woodalls.com. Phone: 805-667-4100
- If you're an RVer with a dog, you might want to check out the book in the *Woodall's* series titled *Camping and RVing with Dogs*. See the online store at www.woodalls.com.

- *The Next EXIT* book tells you what's just off every exit in the U.S., such as food, gas, camping, and shopping. Website: www.thenextexit.com
- If you go to Alaska, don't leave home without *The Milepost Magazine*, which tells you what to expect every milepost along the Alcon Highway. Website: http://milepost.com/
- The Escapees RV Club has *Escapees* magazine you may find helpful and interesting. Website: www.escapees.com/magazine.asp
- Mail service is available through Escapees. Call toll free 1-800-9896, 888-757-2582, or in Livingston, Texas, call 936-327-8873. You can also register online at www.escapees.com.
- Find "The World's Largest Selection of Books, DVDs, eBooks, and More about RVs and the RV Lifestyle" at www.RVbookstore.com.
- Check out www.RVadvice.com for just about anything you'd care to know regarding the RV life. If you don't see what you want to know, you can submit your question for an answer. The site includes definitions of terminology you're likely to encounter in life on the road. RV Advice reports that for the month of October, 2009, the site had more than 37,000 unique visitors.

Things to Take with You

- Toolbox
- First aid kit
- Flashlight*
- Maps
- GPS
- A good working compass
- Cell phone and charger
- Tire gauge
- Hoses: correct size water and sewer hoses
- The RV manual*
- A waterproof safe to hold important information such as passports, if necessary, and titles to your vehicles*
- An extra blanket*
- A phone list of most-called numbers and backup authorities.*
- *Woodall's* campground directory for the area(s) in which you'll be traveling
- Club directories such as *Coast to Coast, Passport America, Western Horizons*

*Also listed in Things We Learned the Hard Way.

- Membership to roadside assistance, such as AAA Plus RV (We've needed this more than once!)
- Optional: inflatable boat. We have the Sea Eagle and a 3.3 hp motor.

  Sea Eagle U.S.A., Division of Hoge Industries, Inc., Port Jefferson, NY 11777. Phone: 1-800-852-0925, or log on to www.seaeagle.com.

Contributors

These are your fellow RVers who have shared their mistakes, mishaps, and adventures on the road. I thank them for taking the time to share so that we might laugh and learn. If you meet them on the road, be sure to thank them, too.

- Farrell and Nancy Adkins
- Jean Anderson
- Dorian and Janis Blake
- David and Christine Budnik
- John and Marcia Carlson
- Joe and Marianne Cavanaugh
- Wayne and Betty Cox
- John and Sandy Fanello
- Ken and Janet Frey
- June Garrison
- Norm and Sue Goulet
- Ken and Rhonda Hardy
- Bill and Darlene Heath
- Herman and Karan Johnson
- Al and Tanny Latuska
- John and Maggie MacFarlane
- John and Sue Mason
- Delores Mason

- Pete McMullen
- Ernie and Helen Menold
- Dan and Laraine Miller
- Curt and Hilda Myers
- Fentar and Jeannine Robbins
- Stewart and Roslyn Schickel

About the Author

Anita S. Henehan was born in St. Louis, Missouri, where she lived until she and her second husband, Paul, bravely sold everything, bought a motor home, and hit the road.

Living in an RV gave Anita a brand new, exciting lifestyle. She and her first husband, Herb Sokolik, had raised three children before a boating accident left her a widow. At age 50, this homemaker launched her first career, founding an art consulting firm. Called Reflections In Design, it provided art to corporations in the U.S. and abroad. After 17 successful years, she sold this business to Color Art and retired "except when former clients call for assistance."

Since May of 2000, Anita and Paul have intermittently traveled North America in their 42-foot motor coach called Merrily We Roll Along Two. Her first book, *How to Run Away from Home After 50*, intrigued thousands who just needed a nudge to "run away" or who've already done so and can laugh in agreement as they read about her adventures. Her new book, *Tales from the Road*, relates more experiences and highlights hilarious episodes, fascinating fiascos, and heartwarming tales contributed by fellow RVers. It also features dozens of favorite places they've traveled in the U.S. and Canada.

Today, Anita volunteers as a tutor at an early childhood school, promotes her books, and travels several months a year in their motor coach. She loves to hear from readers and fellow RVers, and can be reached at 314-308-3785 or henehanmerrily@aol.com.

Quick Order Form

Reflections Publishing
4218 Olive St., St. Louis, MO 63108

Tales from the Road: Adventures of Mid-Life Runaways
By Anita S. Henehan

Three ways to order this book:

1. Telephone: 314-308-3785
2. Clip or copy and mail: see address above
3. Email: henehanmerrily@aol.com

Pricing:

$14.00 per book, plus $4.99 shipping and handling for first book ordered. For each additional book, add $1.25 per book for shipping and handling to the cost of the book/s.

Missouri residents add 8.241% sales tax

Quantity	**Item**	**Cost**	**Amount Due**
_______	*Tales from the Road*	_______	__________
_______	*How to Run Away from Home After 50*	_______	__________
	Shipping and Handling		__________
	Sales tax for Missouri residents 8.241%		__________
		TOTAL	__________

Payment: Make checks payable in U.S. dollars to Anita S. Henehan and mail to the address above. Complete the information below for receiving your order.

Name ____

Address ____

City ______________________ State_______ Zip _________

Phone ____

Email ____

Books will be mailed via Priority Mail (US Postal Service).

Notes

Notes

Notes

Notes

Notes

Notes

Notes

Notes